Cool Careers

CAROLYN BOYES

Collins

First published in the UK in 2008 by Collins
an imprint of HarperCollins*Publishers*
77–85 Fulham Palace Road
London W6 8JB

www.collins.co.uk

A catalogue record for this book is
available from the British Library

ISBN: 978-0-00-726352-3

Set by Rowland Phototypesetting Ltd, Bury St Edmunds, Suffolk

Mixed Sources
Product group from well-managed
forests and other controlled sources
www.fsc.org Cert no. SW-COC-1806
© 1996 Forest Stewardship Council

FSC is a non-profit international organisation established to promote the
responsible management of the world's forests. Products carrying the FSC
label are independently certified to assure consumers that they come
from forests that are managed to meet the social, economic and
ecological needs of present and future generations.

Find out more about HarperCollins and the environment at
www.harpercollins.co.uk/green

Contents

Introduction

Have you ever wanted a different career? Something a little bit different, something fun and exciting? Or that sounds as if it will really keep you interested and happy?

'If you do what you love, you'll never work a day in your life.' Or so the old saying goes. When you have a career you really love doing, your life as a whole becomes immeasurably happier.

David is a lucky man in the eyes of many of his friends. He directs films for a living. It has taken him a long time to find a career he really loves. First he was a barman, then a professional limousine driver, briefly an electrician and, for several years, a cameraman and freelance assistant director. Finally, he started making music videos as a freelance director and now he makes films. The world of film is undoubtedly cool but, more importantly, *he* thinks it's cool. For many years he followed a career path that wasn't exciting, fun or interesting. Now he is fortunate, or clever enough just to fix his eyes on doing something he truly loves.

Your career, like David's, is for you alone. A cool career will transcend the mere idea of work and become a job that you can be really passionate about. There really are no obstacles out there that you can't find your way around. You have to love what you do and go for what you want to do in your life.

Cool Careers contains lots of ideas for some of the coolest and most fascinating careers on the planet right now. There are thousands of careers out there. Most conventional career guides only touch on the headline careers. The aim of *Cool Careers* is to tease out the little ones . . . the interesting jobs that you usually only discover when you have been working for a while.

It is not always easy to decide what career you might like. How should you make the decision? Based on what your friends do? Based on what you have done in your life so far? On your current qualifications or skills?

Well, if you are content with any old job, so be it. But if, on the other hand, you are looking for a career that will keep you fascinated, then this is the book for you.

This book came about because, over the last ten years, I have met hundreds of people who were seeking a career. I kept being asked the same question, 'How do I find a truly satisfying career?'

Some were graduates taking their first steps on the career ladder. Some had lost their job and needed a new one. Many, though, had already held down a job or two before realising that they want something bigger, perhaps better paid, different, more exciting, with more free time or more of a challenge. Many simply felt that their career didn't really express who they were. They just knew something wasn't right.

In other words, what they were looking for was not just any old career but a really *cool* career.

What is a cool career?

Undoubtedly, there are some careers that lots of people in the world think are cool. Others are only considered cool by a select few.

A cool career is basically a career that is in a cool area or is simply cool itself. It is a career that is 'a little bit more' or 'much more' off the beaten track than the average.

Anybody can get a career. However, if you are creative or unconventional, if you want to do what you love and maybe even inspire others to do what they love, you probably are really looking for a *cool* career.

If so, look no further. This book contains *around 500 of the coolest careers in existence today.*

How do I use this book?

Cool Careers is deliberately not laid out like a conventional career guide, even though it contains plenty of ideas to stimulate your thinking about your future career.

This is not an A to Z career guide. A career is not simply something you should pick off the shelf like a tin of baked beans. It is what you are going to spend most of your time doing for the rest of your life!

Yes, you can find lists of careers here. Yes, you can find guidance and career definitions. But you will also find ways of thinking about career choices that are deliberately random and unstructured in order to stimulate your thinking about what matters to you in making your own choice.

Part One of the book takes a brief look at why and how you might find your own cool career – particularly in a rapidly moving global culture. Part Two is full of lists. The lists are selected to fit only one criteria – the areas they cover, and the careers they contain, are cool. See what catches your eye. Pick the book up, scan through it and get some ideas for what you want to do. You can read it all the way through or dip into the odd list.

This is not a definitive guide to every career out there, just the coolest around. Take your time, stimulate your thinking, come up with your own ideas and go and find yourself a really cool career ...

Part One

Is it time for a cool career?

So what is cool?

How many of the following words would you use to describe your thoughts and feelings about your current choice of career?

Exciting
Aspirational
Free
Fun
Happy
Easy
Love
Unusual
Powerful
Challenging
Totally me
Joyful
Profitable

If you don't think any of the above apply, you definitely don't have a cool career. If you do, you think it's cool, and it shouldn't really matter whether other people do too.

Cool careers

You will find many examples of cool careers in the lists in Part Two of the book. Every one of these careers is being done by somebody somewhere. Some careers are so unusual that there is only one person in the world with that job title. Others are derivations of more normal careers, with a twist that makes them much cooler.

Am I ready to be cool?

In each chapter there are examples of careers within the area with varying degrees of cool. It's up to you how cool a career you choose to pursue. You may agree or disagree with the classifications. It's true that cool is a very subjective idea. It doesn't matter if your friends think that you are making eccentric or frivolous choices – let your deepest interests guide you.

Types of career cool

Some areas of work are themselves so cool that any career within them qualifies as a cool career. Creative careers are cool simply because of rarity value; not all of us are creative, so having any creative career is to be recognised as a member of an exclusive club. More recently, green or ethical careers are seen as being very cool.

However, a cool career doesn't have to be fashionable to be cool. *You* are ultimately the judge. Difference, exclusivity, eccentricity or an ordinary career in an obscure location can all be enough.

Do I have a cool career?

Possibly – you may indeed have a cool career right now. There is ultimately only one way to know. When you have a cool career, you'll be proud to tell people what you do at parties. You'll be one of those people others come up to and say, 'Can you help me get a job like yours?' And, more often than not, 'How did you find out about that career – you lucky *!@@@'"'$%^&*?' At which, of course, you will just nod sagely . . . and quietly hand them your copy of *Cool Careers*.

Why do you need a cool career?

COOL CAREERS ARE SO THIS CENTURY

In communist China in the 20th century there was an expression to describe the idea of a job for life – the 'iron rice bowl'. You turned up for work, didn't always do much but got paid, turned up again, and again, and again, retired, and died. Great for filling in time, but not very cool.

That was the extreme side of work but, even in most of the capitalist West, your parents and grandparents could expect a long career without the need to find a new job. The arrival of the 21st century has changed this world of work. Most of us will have numerous jobs during our lifetime. The conventional career structure with its planned, regular promotions and salary rises is disappearing. This has led to loss of security for many, but, at the same time, does allow us all to get more creative about our careers.

Many of the jobs out there didn't exist twenty, ten or even two or three years ago. Some may be variations of existing jobs that have been given a modern twist.

For example, there have always been private detectives, but not until recently internet detectives doing purely internet-based investigations. There have always been interior designers, but how many in the past specialised in using feng shui principles in their work?

START THINKING COOL

The 21st century workplace is an arena of uncertainty. The modern workplace will continue to shift and change as new opportunities open up all over the world and new technologies change the shape of companies and careers.

You will need to learn new skills throughout your life and be in charge of your own self-development. Although companies will invest in training their employees, you will be expected to add value in return, keeping up with the pace of change. You are likely to change employers so, even if you are employed, think of yourself as your own self-employed business.

What we want from work is changing too. More of us expect fulfilment at work; we want to be stimulated. If we are bored we will just change careers. Self-realisation is also big this century. Many of us want work–life balance or autonomous work. Some of us want it all, and now: wealth, power and happiness. We have to be prepared to learn skills in our spare time as well as at work to achieve high employability.

All this adds up to the arrival of new types of career. Not all of them are cool, but some of them are very cool!

Ten good reasons why you need a cool career right now

Change is afoot. If you don't take these factors into account when thinking about your career you could get left behind in a dead-end job or, worse still, become unemployable.

1. **Only you are in charge of your career.** This is the age of self-responsibility. We each need to take charge of our careers. A career for life will no longer be handed to us on a plate. You need a career you can really embrace with gusto and commitment.

2. **Building a lifetime brand – you, inc.** Think carefully about every choice you make. Your career choices sell you not only on your experience but, in effect, as a brand. Your CV is not a history of your background as much as a personal marketing document. The cooler the careers on your CV, the more you will be worth as a 'name-brand' in the market place – this will give you longevity and reward in your career.

3. **Your expectations.** We expect our personal life to provide us with enjoyment and meaning. This has now extended to work-life. A good pay cheque alone is no longer sufficient as a measurement of personal satisfaction. Our own personal definition of coolness is part of the package we expect to get with our jobs.

4. **New working patterns and opportunities.** Nine to five working days are no longer the norm for the whole workforce. There are new ways of working that allow more portfolio careers, short-term contracting, interim employment, telework and self-employment. This gives you more opportunities to choose a cool career.

5. **New technologies.** Technology is cool. It has given us all the flexibility and freedom to work from home as well as from an office. It has also potentially given us more control over our own time and allowed each of us to be more creative and expressive. We can write our own blogs, set up small businesses on the internet and communicate overseas. It is only in the last few years, for example, that people have actually been able to make their living as eBay traders.

6. **Growth of the service economy.** The changes in the West towards service-based economies allow us to create new services for others that have not previously been thought of. Who would have thought a few years ago that personal concierge services for the megarich could provide a career? The fastest growing industries could be, for example, personal services, leisure, business and financial services, hospitality and health care. What career could you choose to fit the trends of this century?

7. **Personal meaning.** This century's expectation is that we 'should' and 'can' express our own values

and interests in the work we do. If we can't, we
generally expect to change jobs. Choose a
career that you consider cool. That choice *is*
available to you.

8. **Self-empowerment and lifelong learning are
valued.** The expectation now exists that we can,
and will, change career more than once, so we
gain the ability to develop different skills by
working in more than one environment or
industry. It is OK to choose not just one, but
several, cool careers that appeal to you.

9. **You are a business.** Working in a big, hierarchical
company no longer needs to be the norm. We
can all set ourselves up as independent
entrepreneurs providing a service to others.
Ideas and creativity will lead you to establish your
unusually cool career.

10. **Globalisation.** The 21st-century world is one of
international movement. We no longer need to
work only in the country we grew up in. We can
have flexible career plans that include a period of
experience overseas that will be valued when we
return home. Broaden your thinking. *Cool
Careers* is full of ideas that will take you across
the world rather than just on a short commute to
a dull grey office block. Think laterally, and find a
very cool career.

PASSING THE PARTY TEST

The easiest way to recognise that you have a cool career is the party test. If you say what you do at a party, and the person you are talking to says, 'Cool!' (or an equivalent exclamation), looks impressed, begins to get a little competitive with you (because they haven't got a cool career like yours), or starts telling everyone else at the party about your career, you know it's cool.

IF YOU'RE NOT PROUD, IT ISN'T COOL

Practise on yourself. Are you proud to tell people what you do, or do you feel the need to lie? Lying is a serious sign that something needs to change fast. Why not really go and get that job you've told the good-looking girl/guy you have? Life's too short to do the same as everyone else.

If you are still not sure, measure your career against the Coolometer.

The Coolometer

The Coolometer is an invention that measures just how cool your career is. Of course, classifications are subjective, and I haven't been scientific about it, because there are some types of job that demand a completely different classification of their own – but through the book I have categorised careers in several ways.

Uncool Neither particularly unusual, nor highly aspirational. If someone asks you what you do, they know immediately what this career is when you mention it. The conversation falters. Watch out for signs of boredom in your audience: fidgeting, folded arms or a sudden need to find a drink. Not covered in this book.

Classic cool Well-recognised as a sought-after career. Classically cool careers sometimes take specialist training before you can do them, or may be particularly competitive to get in to. May gain you a friend at a party.

Very cool A more unusual career. A very cool career may be a specialist or sub-category of a classically cool career or a related niche career. Mentioning that you do this career at a party is bound to start an interesting conversation. There is very unlikely to be anyone else in the room with your career.

Unusually cool There are many careers that are one-offs, 21st-century only careers, or available only in a particular geographical location. An unusually cool career might even be a career that didn't exist until you made it up. To find an unusually cool career, keep your eyes peeled for new careers in the newspapers and on television. Think about what you could add to your career to make it more interesting and more unusual. You will be the talk of the party.

How to build a cool career

Some of us find cool careers straight away. Others may need to develop a cool career out of a so-so start. The cooler the career you are after, the more unconventional it will be by our definition. As a result, you aren't going to find this kind of career by looking in the obvious places. You need to take your time and really think about what you want.

BLAZE YOUR OWN TRAIL

People with cool careers are unconventional. They blaze their own trail in life. They decide what they really want and they choose a career that is likely to give it to them.

Expect to have a different life from the majority of people that you know. Perhaps you will travel more, meet more eccentric people, work different hours, but you should also have far more fun than everyone else you know. If what you do also makes for good conversation, even better.

To begin to decide on your own cool career, you will have to become your own career detective.

Five steps to decide who you are and what you want

1. **Look at your interests.** What do you enjoy doing?

   - Are there any particular activities or subjects that keep your interest? These might be a hobby rather than a work interest at present.
   - Do you have a real passion for any area of life? Forget at the moment whether or not you have any training in relation to the area. Simply think about what you enjoy doing. Here are some examples: the environment, playing computer games, cars and mechanical objects, influencing people, travel, science, helping others, directing and leading, changing the world, doing something personal and meaningful, collecting data or objects, writing or artistic pursuits.

- When you think about what you really love, what career direction does that start to point you towards?

2. **Get to know yourself.** Take a long, hard look at your personality. Be honest with yourself. Your work is going to take up a huge part of your life. There is no point pretending to be someone you are not.

   - Are you a completer/finisher who always delivers tasks on time? Or perhaps you are much more a big picture, philosopher type who is great at ideas and strategic thinking.
   - Maybe you are a moody, artistic type who is wonderful at living in your imagination? Ask your friends for their opinion if you are not sure.
   - Psychometric profiling tools, such as MBTI (Myers-Briggs Type Indicator), or specific career profiling tools, such as the Holland typing systems, are very effective for revealing your character traits. You may have to pay a career counsellor to help you but it could be worth it. If you are short of cash, there is a lot of information online if you search under the tools' names.
   - Choose a job that suits what you are naturally good at rather than trying to change yourself to suit the job. Changing yourself will neither make you rich nor happy. Doing a job that suits your personality, on the other hand, will.

3. **Look at your current skills.** How many steps are you away from your ideal career right now?

   - What skills would you need to learn or train in to make your ideal career a reality?
   - What would it take for you to learn these skills?
   - Is it physically possible for you to learn them? For example, if you are already 70, it's probably too late for you to be a Premiership footballer, but you might still be able to create yourself a career to do with football.

4. **Decide what's important.** What is really important to you in your career?

   - Is it money? Status? Flexible hours? Security and a nine-to-five routine? Regular promotions? Adventure and excitement?
   - Perhaps you want to be your own boss?
   - Maybe you need company, or would you prefer to be by yourself most of the time?
   - Is location is a key factor?
   - Do you want to work in an office, or outside?
   - Would you like to dress up for work and look glamorous, or never have to put on a suit or smart dress?

5. **Look around at what other people do.** Other people's jobs and career paths can be the inspiration that you need to think about your own career choices. Unconventional careers are comparatively rare so it is important to keep your eyes peeled.

- Who is currently doing the job you really want to do?
- Who is doing a job in an industry or area that you would really like to work in?
- How did they get that job?

Ten steps to getting a cool career

Introspection is a good first step but it will get you nowhere if you don't take action. We only create change by both thinking *and* acting ourselves into new roles before we take them on. If you are looking for an unconventional career, you need some unconventional strategies to help you find it.

1. NETWORK, NETWORK, NETWORK

Networking is the best way to gather information about unusual and unconventional careers. Most of the conventional job market is hidden. The unconventional job market is even more hidden. Search out success stories. Find out who are the top people in your chosen field, or role models who can teach you new things. Find ways to meet them. Don't expect to find them in your existing social network. Break out of your existing social habits and meet new people. Remember the Six Degrees of Separation theory – we are each of us only six people away from anyone in the world. If you contact a friend they can put you in touch with another friend who can give you another contact and so on down the line until you meet the person you really want to get in touch with. Do your research and ask questions all along the way about what interesting careers are out there and how you could get started in your career of choice.

2. THINK CREATIVELY

Take the path less travelled. There may not be one career that suits you but several that will suit you at different times. If you have the chance, volunteer or do short contracts, trying out different jobs as much as possible. Each of them will teach you more about what you like and dislike. Remember, in this century we can invent our own careers by taking bits of different careers and giving them a new title.

3. LIVE WITH CONTRADICTIONS

If you can't find the perfect career straight away, that's OK. Just keep taking step after step and make sure each step is consistent with your values, personality and interests. As you build self-knowledge by taking action, inspiration about different career paths you could follow will come along.

4. KEEP FLEXIBLE

Remember, we are each of us more than one person. What interests you at one time in your life may not be right for you at another. Be prepared to be flexible and respond to your intuition as to when to change paths.

5. FAILURE IS OK

It is perfectly OK to have a career on your CV that wasn't right for you. Trial and error teaches us more than intro-spection. As you learn more about yourself, you can get more precise and accurate in matching your career choices to who you are.

6. TAKE SMALL STEPS TO GET YOU TO THE BIG GOAL

Even if you know what your ideal career is, it may take a while – even years – to get there. Although it would be wonderful to wave a magic wand, small wins are the best ways to work the path towards a bigger goal. Use each small change you make, and everything you learn, as feedback about what you want and how to get your big goal. Accept that the path often weaves in and out of rocks and dis-appears for a while underground before coming back again. It is not a straight line. A series of small wins will add up to a big change over time.

7. KEEP LEARNING

If you don't have the opportunity to learn through your current job and you can't afford to take an immediate leap to another career, identify voluntary or parallel projects that you could take on that will give you new skills or insights. Turning points in careers don't usually come because of one huge leap, but because of a build-up of preferences and commitment from different assignments over time. It is better to spend more time trying out different ways or styles of working in extracurricular projects, where you can afford to change direction, rather than taking a huge career leap that might prove hard to reverse and cost you money or security.

8. BE PATIENT

Career growth and transition take time. If you want to take the unfamiliar path, it may take two, three, or even more, years for you to grow the career you really want.

9. RECOGNISE OPPORTUNITIES WHEN THEY APPEAR

We all have periods when we make progress and periods when we seem to get stuck. Always keep your eyes peeled for opportunities. Career chances don't always come conveniently labelled as such. Keep your eyes open for opportunities to make your career cooler than it is at present. Think about becoming an expert in a particular niche area. Or how about changing geographical location? What are you prepared to do that other people might not consider? Make a story out of your career so far. Take advantage of whatever life throws at you. Only you can make your career a positive experience for you. Tell the story of your life in a positive way to bring meaning to your career and it will make you get clear on the next steps you can take.

10. TAKE A RISK AND BECOME SELF-EMPLOYED

You can aim for an employed career or you can just get your name out there and invent your own. Be prepared to take a risk and go self-employed once you really know your own working preferences. It takes some courage but it could be your best investment in yourself ever. Check out the unusual careers in the lists in Part Two for ideas about one-off careers.

Turning uncool into very cool

Don't panic if you have just realised that you are very uncool. With a little creativity you can start developing your career into a cool career. It's up to you just how cold you want to go.

EXAMPLE 1: A COOL ADRENALIN CHARGED CAREER

Classic cool: Pilot Being a pilot is an example of a classically cool career. Pilots have status. Little boys grow up wanting to be them. But the amount of cool depends on what type of pilot you are. A **Commercial Pilot** is a much sought-after career – aspirational, but not particularly unusual.

Very cool: an RAF Pilot Might score extra Cool points. Why? Fewer people have the opportunity to become RAF pilots. The tough training programme and reputation for 'Top Gun' adrenalin-charged flying produces extra cool points for many.

Think laterally to find a cool career: A linked **very cool** career is **Air Traffic Controller**. It requires quick reflexes and a high degree of skill, as well as a cool, calm character.

Unusually cool: a Seaplane Pilot In the golden age of the 1930s and 1940s, seaplanes complete with smoking lounges and cocktail bars would fly around the British Empire, but they are much rarer nowadays. A new seaplane school has recently been set up in Glasgow but there are likely to be only a handful of seaplanes flying in the whole of the UK in the next five years. The exclusivity of being a seaplane pilot creates an **unusually cool** classification. (If you want to find out more contact the UK Seaplane Association.)

EXAMPLE 2: A COOL CREATIVE CAREER

Classic cool: Singer There are many types of singer, from backing to nightclub to opera. Some have low-paying jobs; others find fame and fortune. If you specialise in one type of music, or have a fantastic vocal range, there is work in recording studios, musicals, the theatre and opera.

Very cool: Singer (niche) How about developing a line in overtone singing, English folk, Gregorian chanting, Mongolian folk or country and western? If you are one of the few people in an area with a skill, you are likely to open up a nice niche in the market.

EXAMPLE 3: A COOL CAREER USING YOUR BODY

So-so: Sports/physical activity teacher/trainer This is an average career. There are plenty of careers around in this area. It may be an enjoyable career, but not particularly aspirational in terms of monetary or status rewards. There are lots of ways you can teach a physical activity – in a school or college, in a club, in a gym.

Classic cool: Trainer in yoga/pilates/martial arts You can up your cool factor by choosing an unusual speciality within the same field. Some of the classically coolest right now are yoga, pilates, martial arts. Keep an eye out for the latest fashions in fitness to become even cooler.

Very cool: niche opportunities in personal training How about giving training in Israeli self-defence for an additional cool factor. Or take a dance class in Bollywood Bangra? Or how about being a **celebrity personal trainer**? While being a personal trainer in the average gym isn't going to win you many 'cool' points, thinking laterally and changing your geographical location rather than your job title can have the same effect of upping your cool. Make a move to Beverly Hills or Los Angeles, get yourself a DVD and an agent, a celebrity endorsement and some good PR and suddenly you become very cool indeed.

In fact, thinking ambitious and being prepared to move to an exciting or unusual part of the world can make many careers cooler.

EXAMPLE 4: A PEOPLE CAREER

So-so: Counsellors Being a counsellor is not very rare nowadays. You don't have to have a psychology background to train as a counsellor, e.g. as a relationship counsellor. Think how you could make it a little cooler, though.

Classic cool: Counselling psychologist Extra cool points come from the fact that this requires more training and so is rarer. You will help individuals understand and take action to overcome their problems to promote well-being. Counselling psychologists believe that behaviour is affected by a person's environment, including family, social issues and psychological issues in the individual. They may also teach and do research with individuals, organisations or groups.

Classic cool: Rehabilitation psychologists They help victims of accidents and developmental disabilities, such as autism, deal with everyday life, including areas such as pain management. They may also work as expert witnesses in legal investigation into the effect of a disability on a person's ability to work.

Very cool: Police profilers Use their understanding of criminals and psychology to catch the bad guys.

Unusually cool: An **Expert in serial killers** takes their understanding a little bit further and uses research to create a really unusually cool career.

EXAMPLE 5: A PRECISE AND DETAILED CAREER

Classic cool: Doctor Being a doctor is cool. Not all of us could qualify, it takes years of training and hopefully provides a lifetime of status in the community and good financial rewards.

Very cool: Plastic surgeons are almost celebrities nowadays. Being a plastic surgeon is cool. However, being a female plastic surgeon is more rare and so, arguably, cooler.

Unusually cool: Australian bush doctor It may not provide you with the same financial rewards, but working in the Australian bush will bring you excitement and variety. The location and adrenalin make this career unusually cool.

Finally

We hope that, whatever you do currently, the career lists in Part Two will inspire you to think about what you really want to do. Fire up your imagination and get thinking about careers you may never have considered, or even heard of, before.

Enjoy finding your new cool career!

Part Two

1. In the know

What could be cooler than knowing about things before everyone else? Throw in a little adventure, travel to exotic places and your career will be top of the party gossip.

Here are a bunch of cool careers for people who like to get to the bottom of events, gossip, or uncover international, criminal or business secrets.

I can keep a secret

Going undercover has to be one of the coolest types of careers around. But it is not just James Bond. There are undercover jobs across a range of industries.

You'll need to:

- Be good at keeping your work confidential – you probably won't be able to talk much about what your job involves
- Be keen on adventure and risk
- Be able to keep calm even in the midst of some uncomfortable circumstances.

If you still want to go undercover to nail the bad guys, carry on.

COOL UNDERCOVER

Environmental Crime Investigator — These investigators usually work for government agencies; they search out people who have broken environmental laws. This could mean a company dumping waste or carrying out activities that are hazardous to human health. As rules become more stringent, this is set to be a growing profession.

Private Investigator — Private investigators carry out a range of investigations, including surveillance, security consultancy, insurance fraud investigations, and matrimonial/partner investigations (fidelity). This is a growth market because of the number of lawsuits nowadays. Store detective work can be a good place to start this career.

Corporate Investigator — Corporate investigators carry out due diligence, covert surveillance and a range of investigations into areas such as fraud, substance abuse investigations, computer forensics, workers' compensation fraud, sexual harassment allegations, and accidents.

Legal Investigator — In the USA, particularly, there is a growing market for legal investigators who are trained to work with court cases for law firms. They may analyse evidence, collect witness statements, help to prepare defence cases and carry out background investigations on anyone involved in the court case. Some may be called on to give evidence in court.

Financial Investigator — Financial investigators have developed a speciality in investigating banking and financial fraud cases. Some may be forensic or Certified Public Accountants (CPAs), or they may have a background in banking or a related industry. White-collar fraud is a growing area and **Banking compliance** may be a useful background for this career. Money may be moved internationally so it is important to thoroughly understand the international financial systems.

Mystery Shopper — A mystery shopper works for an external consultancy and secretly tries out services as a member of the public and rates the service they receive. As well as customer satisfaction services, they may also check on staff compliance with regulations, security and training needs, and benchmark a company against its competitors.

Undercover Narcotics/Drugs Agent — Undercover agents and deep-cover officers work for institutions such as the police and customs. They carry out surveillance, undercover activities and searches. Clearly it can be a risky career and one you are not likely to get into without a lot of training and experience in other related areas.

* *UNUSUALLY COOL*

Undercover Animal Rights Investigator –
You may not get paid directly to do this, but, if you have a passion for animals, you could work undercover for an organisation like PETA, infiltrating industries that use animals for experiments, fur or food, and documenting any abuses or cruelty. Armed with a notepad or secret camera, undercover investigators have been remarkably successful in producing material to be used by campaigners. You must be able to keep accurate notes, stay within the law, keep secrets, be good at building working relationships and if need be, be able to observe animal suffering while staying objective.

I want to be the first to know

What's really going on? Do you like to be the first one to know? Would you like to have information that the majority of the population can't get hold of?

If you want to have an investigative career, you'll need a good memory and an eye for detail, as well as a curious mind. Natural investigators love 'being in the know', they like to have the facts before others do. Their inquisitiveness will lead them down alleyways others don't even notice.

These careers use the mind rather than muscle but they are always interesting and sometimes fast-paced and exciting.

COOL AND CALCULATING

Political Journalist — As either a print (newspapers and magazine) or broadcast journalist, focusing on life in Westminster or Washington, you'll be privy to gossip and secrets, only some of which you'll be able to pass on to the public.

Financial/Business Journalist — Perhaps the secrets of what a company is doing what is more your thing? If so, take a look at the work of the financial or business correspondent. However, if you want to be even earlier to the business stories, it might be worth considering working as a **Financial/Investment Analyst** — for either an investment management or a stockbroking house. Analysts keep in regular contact with a group of companies and need to be up to date on growth forecasts and developments, so they are often among the first people to know what's really going on.

Foreign Correspondent — Stationed overseas, from Gaborone to Hong Kong, you'll interview everyone from the heads of state, to local activists and chairs of industry, chasing down stories of interest to your audience at home. The major TV stations, national newspapers and news-wire organisations all employ overseas correspondents. However, you will probably have honed your news skills in many other posts first.

Undercover Reporter — An undercover reporter may work for a newspaper, magazine or a TV documentary production company. Generally a great deal of experience is called for. You need to be cool in a crisis and an experienced journalist, who is well-versed on the boundaries of what is, and is not, legally possible. You may work near to home or be required to go overseas. This is a dangerous career. You could end up getting on the wrong side of some nasty people.

Corporate Risk Management Specialists — Often also corporate investigators, these specialists assess risk and carry out security surveys. They may provide executive protection, security services and technical surveillance countermeasures. They need to have details about exactly what is going on in a country and the day-to-day changes in risk.

Security Consultant — If you are ex-army, secret service or police, or speak many languages, you might find employment in the private part of the security industry in areas such as kidnapping, insurance, intelligence gathering and security. Look at companies such as Control Risks in the UK or CTC in the States to see the type of work on offer.

* *UNUSUALLY COOL*

MI5 intelligence Officer –

Intelligence officers carry out surveillance operations, run agents, assess and investigate threats to national security or carry out other general management work. They generally work as part of a team. MI5 officers must hold a British passport and the recruitment and vetting process can take at least six months. If you have a second language, you may also work in intelligence work with the service. MI5 has a website that shows current opportunities. **MI5 Data Analysts** analyse trends in electronic data.

Psychic Investigator –

Psychic and paranormal investigators seek to uncover whether or not hauntings and poltergeist phenomena are genuine. Some are sceptics who want to disprove phenomena. Others may carry out 'psychic clearings'. They use a variety of methods ranging from the scientific and cynical to the use of self-proclaimed mediums and psychics, depending on the organisation. Research and university-based organisations require scientific training. Independent companies are not necessarily accredited.

Alien/UFO Investigator –

There are a number of independent and scientific organisations researching stories of aliens, alien abduction and UFOs. In a similar vein, investigators of crop circles, cattle mutilations and other phenomena are also popular. Curiosity is clearly a must. Scientific knowledge would theoretically be useful. A related career requiring greater training is astrobiology – these scientists investigate the origin of life on planets.

I want to get to grips with evidence

One appealing area for those who want a cool career that gets to the bottom of things is forensics. The word 'forensic' comes from the Latin *forensis*, meaning a court or forum.

A forensic practitioner is someone who gives evidence as an expert in court proceedings. These careers combine an ability to get to grips with evidence, a concentration on detail and skill as a good public speaker.

INVESTIGATIVE COOL

Computer Forensics Specialist — This is a growing profession because of the need to protect businesses from a range of computer abuses, including intellectual property theft and fraud. A computer forensics specialist recovers deleted, encrypted or damaged files, tracks internet files, and investigates illegal, inappropriate or threatening email communications. The evidence may be used for litigation in civil and criminal cases involving areas such as embezzlement or pornography, or in workplace theft investigations.

Forensic Speech Consultant — Forensic speech consultants analyse speech and voice to identify who the speaker is. This career may involve carrying out voice line-ups and voice identification, comparison and elimination in criminal cases. They may also get involved as an expert in verifying transcripts of speech.

Forensic Pathologist — The forensic pathologist epitomised by the TV character Quincy carries out autopsies for the coroner as part of investigations into sudden, violent or unexpected deaths. In the UK you need a background in histopathology and forensic pathology and legal training. Further details about the training path towards forensic pathology can be obtained from the Royal College of Pathologists (www.rcpath.org).

Forensics Explosive Expert — Forensics explosives experts provide evidence in legal cases and insurance work in areas, such as accident reconstruction and crime and terrorism cases. They provide testimony to lawyers and prosecutors as well as government agencies. Forensics experts exist in many areas, for example, maritime accidents, workplace accidents, medical claims and fires. Their work includes reviewing documents and records, site reviews, fire cause and origin investigations, among other areas. Common to these jobs is the ability to analyse evidence, communicate an argument in court and apply scientific techniques practically to an investigation.

Forensic Medical Examiners — Forensic medical examiners carry out routine work, such as the effect of drink and drugs on detained people, and look at victims of assault. They need to be able to present evidence in court and also be expert in examining wounds and other evidence. More details can be obtained from the Association of Police Surgeons (www.apsweb.org.uk). They are also known as forensic physicians or police surgeons. If you like the sound of this, look also at lawyers specialising in medical negligence or medical defence.

Forensic Anthropologist — Forensic anthropologists apply anthropology to the law. As an example, if the police were to find skeletal remains they might ask a forensic anthropologist to identify the deceased. They are also used in human rights abuses, such as war crimes where mass graves have been found, or in cases of other buried evidence.

Criminal Justice Expert — A criminal justice expert will have an investigative agency or legal background and will be involved in writing, consulting and acting as an expert witness in legal matters in areas such as terrorism, drug enforcement, military justices and intelligence cases. They may run training or speak at academic events.

Forensic Psychiatrist — A forensic psychiatrist is a psychiatrist who understands mental disorders and has a working knowledge of the law. They may work in an outpatient capacity in prisons or provide psychiatric reports, and comment on medical and legal issues for the criminal justice system and the Home Office. Some work in the high security hospitals such as Broadmoor. They may also provide advice to adult psychiatric services. Most forensic psychiatrists work in the NHS, although psychiatric patients are also found in the private sector. Similar careers are to be found in forensic psycotherapy, forensic learning disabilities and forensic adolescent psychiatry.

Forensic Botanist — Forensic botanists deal in environmental evidence. They carry out analysis of both plants and soil. For example, they might sample pollen and spores from an object or suspect's clothing to match a particular crime scene and particular geology. These professionals were used in the investigation of mass graves in Srebrenica in the 1990s.

Forensic Accountant — A perfect way to change a so-so career as an accountant into a cool career. Forensic accountants use accountancy, investigative and auditing skills to look at financial evidence for the courts. They are employed by the police, insurance companies, banks, government agencies and independent organisations, and may be used as expert witnesses.

Forensic Psychologist — A forensic psychologist combines an understanding of people with an application to the law. Would you like to know what effect a witness has on a jury or if a defendant has the mental capacity to be tried? You could become an expert witness in court and may even study the law as well to help you develop more expertise in your work. Most forensic psychologists in the UK work for the prison service. However, they can also be found in academia, probation, police and social services. This is also referred to as investigative and criminological psychology.

* *UNUSUALLY COOL*

Forensic Linguist –
Forensic linguists carry out written and spoken textual analysis. For example, they might have to decide whether or not the author of a text is the same as a person who has been accused of a crime, or they might check for plagiarism. They may also be asked to carry out psychological profiling of the author, for example, deciding on the mental state of the author, for criminal, terrorist or insurance fraud purposes.

Phonetician –
This is a related career to a forensic linguist but (forensic) phoneticians analyse only speech. They make comparisons of speakers by accent, dialect, voice quality and other speech features to identify the speaker or to carry out profiling. They also provide evidence on disputed utterances in court and carry out analysis of speech on black box recordings. Police and the secret service need phoneticians, but they are rare in the UK at present – there are less than 50 – though

there are more in other countries. Contact the
International Association of Forensic Phonetics and
Acoustics for more information.

Coroner –
Coroners in England and Wales are independent
judicial officers who are responsible for looking into
and coming up with judgments on violent, sudden and
unexpected, unnatural or suspicious deaths. The
equivalent position in Scotland is the Procurator Fiscal.
Most coroners work on a part-time basis. Some
coroners are lawyers, some are doctors and some have
both qualifications. For further information try
contacting your local coroner.

Forensic Lip-reader –
This is a very new idea in the UK. Professional lip-
readers are used from time to time by journalists to see
what celebrities are saying, but, in the USA, forensic lip-
readers are used as professional witnesses in trials to
review surveillance tapes. They are also sometimes
used to communicate what a patient with speech
difficulties is saying to a doctor.

In the know
Celebrity Starter Careers

Christina Aguilera, like **Britney Spears** and **Justin Timberlake**, gained her first experience as a performer as a child singer in Disney's Mickey Mouse Club.

Woody Allen, the Oscar-winning director, writer and comedian, began writing one-liners for gossip columns aged only 15. He carried on as a comic writer for different television shows, until writing his first feature film in 1962.

2. Past, Present and Future

Are your feet firmly rooted in the Now? Or maybe the 21st century doesn't do much for you? Perhaps you would rather spend each day living in a bygone era – or dreaming about an age that hasn't yet come. It's cool to choose 'when' to work as well as where to work. What career will you choose? Past, present or future?

I like to live in the future

Are you a trendspotter or a trendsetter? Do you enjoy forecasting future needs? Perhaps you enjoy spotting potential risks or threats? If so, consider a career that enables you to live in the future. They are all very cool.

VERY COOL

Horizon Scanning Analyst — Horizon scanning is the systematic examination of potential threats and opportunities in a particular area over a three- to ten-year period. As an analyst working for a government department or big organisation, you will anticipate future trends and challenges arising, for example, from new technologies, working practices or political developments.

Futurologist/Futurist — May also use horizon scanning or other techniques. You will analyse trends and guess what we will be doing in the future, or provide long-range planning and scenario development. Futurologists are found advsing on global trends, risk management and consumer market opportunities in industries such as psychology, computer science, anthropology, political science and sociology. Also known as **Foresight Consultants**, **Road-mappers**, **Cultural Critics**, **Corporate Strategists**, **Policy Analysts**. Similar skills can be found in **Planners** and **Marketers**.

Flood-risk Specialist — A flood-risk analyst carries out studies into the risk of flooding and prepares flood-risk mapping. They need to understand hydraulic modelling and hydrology and will probably have a civil engineering, water science or physical geography degree. **Risk Analysts** are to be found in many fields including **Credit** and **Business.**

Chief Security Officer — Many global companies engage a chief security officer, who works within a company to ensure the safety of both the company's employees and their assets. They must be able to analyse future threats from all directions, be it terrorism or local unrest overseas, and they coordinate security at global offices. They need good contacts in law enforcement and intelligence agencies. They also play a key business role, analysing business decisions and their implications for the board and the CEO.

Climatologist — A climatologist studies long-term trends in the world's climate. While meteorologists study what is likely to happen to the weather in the short term, climatologists may look at trends and patterns over millennia, as well as the natural or human factors that may cause climate change.

Medium/Psychic — A psychic or medium predicts what will happen in a person's future through clairvoyance, aura reading and spirit communication. Institutions do offer psychic and medium training.

Tarot Reader — Tarot readers and tarot therapists use the tarot deck of cards to tell the future, and also, on occasion, to counsel or coach. Anyone can, in theory, set up as a self-employed tarot reader. You need to understand the meanings of the cards and to have some natural psychic abilities and sensitivity to people. There are an increasing number of companies offering web-based services.

* *UNUSUALLY COOL*

Cryonics Scientist –
Cryonics is the practice of preserving humans and animals after death for some undefined point in the future at which they might be able to be resuscitated. At present there are two institutes, in Arizona and in Michigan, which practise this on a large scale.

Volcanologist –
A volcanologist predicts whether or not a volcano is in danger of eruption in the future. Their skills can directly save lives. A PhD in geology is vital, since geology provides the knowledge of how volcanic materials react with air and water. Very few places offer volcanology as a study and it is a dangerous profession. You could get killed on the job by magma or volcanic flows. Similar skills may be used in areas such as ecology, geology, oceanography, glaciology and hydrology.

20 ways to leave a legacy

For the very future-orientated, it is possible to choose a career that will involve not looking into the future but, in some way, living on into the future. What do you want your legacy to be? Will it be a business or a product that will stand the test of time? Perhaps you want to leave a foundation or charitable organisation as your legacy. Maybe it will be a piece of art or even a policy that you have influenced.

Many of us start out on our career paths wanting to change the world by our presence in it. If you want to make an impact that outlasts your life on this planet, consider all the ways you can leave a lasting legacy for future generations. Here are 20 careers that others have used to change the world for generations to come.

1. Artist

2. Sculptor

3. Film-maker

4. Archivist

5. Inventor

6. Fiction writer

7. Politician

8. Political activist

9. Anti-slavery/human rights campaigner

10. Conservationist

11. Software/computer developer

12. Physicist

13. Chemist

14. Doctor

15. Philanthropist

16. Transplant surgeon (think of all the firsts in surgery!)

17. Spiritual leader

18. Pharmaceutical drug developer

19. Architect

20. Business founder

I like to live in the past

We are becoming a nosy nation. There is a big growth in personal heritage and the industry of the past. People want to know the history of where they have lived, who their ancestors were and what they did. If you love precision work there is ample scope in the conservation and heritage field. If you prefer research, look at specialising in a historical era or a field such as genealogy. Or perhaps you would like to re-create a look or product of the past?

CLASSIC COOL

Biographer — Biographers research and write about individuals, alive or dead, using sources such as news archives, letters, diaries and interviews with people who knew the subject. A biographer needs an eye for a good narrative and an understanding of psychology and character. Ideas may come from your publisher, your own sources and interests, or from the subject themselves.

Art Restorer — Art restorers clean and repair valuable artworks in order to preserve the life of the object or painting. They work for museums, members of the public, the heritage industry and antique dealers. Attention to detail is important as the works are often very fragile. Restorers must also be knowledgeable about art history and apply this knowledge to their work. You will need to work with tools and the latest technologies, such as digital imaging equipment. You can enter this profession through a professional apprenticeship or a City and Guilds qualification. Being a **Conservation Officer** is a similar profession.

Family/Gene Detective — Otherwise known as a genealogist, in this career you will need to have a passion for research. There are no formal qualifications but a knowledge of palaeography (ancient script) is essential. It is also important to know some Latin. Most genealogists are self-employed. Some teach and a few work for specialist research companies.

Archivist — An archivist manages and organises historical records and archives. This may involve conservation of documents and appropriate storage. Archivists need to be methodical, interested in history and good at dealing with enquiries from the public. Contact the Society of Archivists for more information.

Heritage Manager — A heritage manager is responsible for the conservation and management of one or more heritage sites. They may have project management backgrounds. Heritage sites include buildings, ancient monuments and prehistoric sites and landscapes. A manager may be asked to develop visitor attractions, secure funding or find other ways of generating income, for example providing film locations.

Archaeological Conservator — Archaeological conservators protect artefacts from deterioration and damage. They identify, record and clean fragile objects and materials for long-term storage. They may work on site but tend to be based in museums or universities, though some are self-employed. They have specialist knowledge of historical periods and the properties of particular materials and environments.

VERY COOL

Heraldry Specialist — Heraldry is the study of coats of arms. It has been around for 700 years and has developed its own language. Heraldry specialists trace and decide on what coats of arms can be used by an individual. They also carry out family research. The College of Arms is the official British repository of the coats of arms and pedigrees of families and their descendants (though it does not include Scottish families).

Vintage Car Specialist — A vintage car specialist may be a dealer of cars, hire cars for TV or film productions, or be a restorer of vintage cars specialising in a particular make. There are also specialists in classic and vintage car insurance, accessories and other services.

Historical Costume Designer — A historical costume designer researches, designs and makes costumes from a particular period. They may also have expertise in materials. They work for museums and other collections, as well as in the TV, film and theatre world. A design background is the norm.

* *UNUSUALLY COOL*

House Detective –

House detectives or house historians research the history of properties. They may look at private houses or public buildings, such as palaces or castles in the UK or overseas. If you want to set yourself up in this newly popular area, it would be useful to have a background in research, scientific analysis, architecture or archaeology.

I want to do something this century

Twenty-first century ways of working and globalisation are opening up new opportunities for making money in non-traditional ways and other careers are coming into existence for the first time. If you want a very modern career, keep an eye on the news and trends for both people and new technology.

VERY COOL

ebay Trader — eBay has now become so well known and well used globally that many people try to make a living as professional e-traders. It is possible, as long as you follow certain rules. Practice makes perfect. Decide first on your niche. Do you want to specialise? Or sell just anything? If you want this to be your career, make sure you deliver: ratings are everything. Be aware also that anyone trading for profit has to register for tax. You can find a guide for online trading at www.hmrc.gov.uk/findout.

Virtual Reality Entreprenur — According to analysts in the US, the market for massively multiplayer online games (MMORPG) is now worth more than $1 billion in the West alone, so there is everything to play for. The market is set to grow by a further third in the next four years. Of course, you can make money by setting up your own virtual world if you are successful in selling your concept. But you can also change virtual reality money into cold hard cash. In 2007, a player became the first virtual world millionaire. The most famous MMORPG is the shared 3D world Second Life. In this virtual world you can create an online version of yourself (called an avatar). Your avatar can do business 'in world' and convert the online currency into real world money.

Professional Blogger — Building a high-traffic website is an appealing way to make money outside the rat race. There are tips aplenty on the internet about how to market and attract traffic to your blog, but here are some basics. Obviously, you need to create original content that will genuinely be of value to others. Decide what you can do that will change people's thinking or life in some way. If you can get results for others your site will be worth visiting. To build traffic to your site, link into other sites, look up social bookmarking sites, and use ad networks and affiliate programs. You can never predict the trends of what will attract the audience's imagination, so the best tactic may be to blog for pleasure and see over time whether you can build your blog from a hobby into an enterprise.

Professional Property Investor — There's no need to go out to work every day if you have the know-how to run your own property development business. Buy-to-let, owning land or commercial property in the UK, or investing overseas can provide you with both income and capital growth, if you pay attention to the trends and can raise capital. Be aware, though, that there are huge risks.

Clutter Clearer — Fifty-six per cent of Britons are self-confessed hoarders. As we cram into smaller dwellings, our consumerism grows and grows. We all have too much stuff. To cope with our clutter obsession, the professional de-junking expert has emerged. If you want to become one, you will probably need to set up your own business. For more information get in touch with the recently set up professional body The Association of Professional Declutterers and Organisers (APDO).

Drug Therapist — Drug rehabilitation is a very 21st-century need, and specialists in drug therapy will be in demand for a long time to come. Psychiatry is clearly a good route into this career.

Cognitive Behavioural Therapist — Sadly, depression is also very prevalent this century. Cognitive Behavioural Therapy (CBT) is one of the most proven ways of combating depression and low self-esteem. You do not need a psychology background to learn the basics.

Humanist Funeral Celebrant — It is now possible to celebrate a funeral with a civil celebrant rather than a member of the clergy. Humanists believe in an ethical approach to life without religion. If you would like to find out more, contact the British Humanist Association.

* UNUSUALLY COOL

Religious Consultant –

A religious consultant advises the public and private sector on a particular religion, and the community who believe in the religion. They may be an adherent of the religion themselves, an academic authority on a number of religions, or a sceptic who is concerned with the effect of certain religions or cults. Clearly there is a growing need for information to bridge the 21st-century secular and religious worlds. If you like the idea of this career you will need to create your own niche or start as a **Religious Journalist**.

I want to have retro cool

These careers are old-fashioned. Some are even ancient. Yet, once again, they are cool in the 21st century.

RETRO COOL

Yoga Teacher/Studio Owner — Yoga is an ancient tradition yet the epitome of 21st-century cool. Yoga studios have grown up all over Britain and hot yoga is just one of the latest incarnations of yoga for the fashionable crowd. Teaching obviously requires dedicated training. However, you could open your own studio and hire in teachers as a relaxing way to make a profit.

Druid/Wiccan Witch/Magician/Shaman — Clearly these are not careers that would suit everyone. But who wants to be everyone? The ancient magical traditions are very cool again. Visit Mind Body and Spirit festivals to find out what's going on, and research the Western mystery traditions. Travel overseas and check out more exotic traditions such as the Kahuna in Hawaii or Shamans in South and Central America. Read Carlos Castaneda or Dion Fortune if you want to get inspired.

Peking Opera/Kabuki Star — The ancient singing arts are very cool ever since Gregorian chanting hit the big time. To become a Peking Opera or Kabuki star you will need to study Chinese or Japanese, unless you can start your own version in English, but use your imagination and search out an equivalent ancient art form nearer home and you could have an extraordinarily cool career.

Pawnbroker — Intriguingly old-fashioned and possibly due for a little retro cool. While the rest of the high street becomes more uniform and dull, pawnbrokers carry on, as they have for centuries, serving a more specialist clientele with cash as needed.

Storyteller — Professional storytellers tell stories to an audience. They believe that the oral tradition and narrative can enhance the lives of an audience. There has been a rebirth of the art over the last three decades. Professional storytellers perform in libraries, in schools and on stage. Now, storytelling has also been taken into the workplace as a tool for making sure good practice is communicated throughout a company.

Rainmaker — Called in to conduct ceremonies to make it rain in dry climates. Usually also known as a shaman. The magical community has been going for thousands of years but they are very 'now' with the growth of the alternative and self-development market.

Bonsai Artist — A bonsai artist or culturist grows small trees in pots. They take ordinary trees and, during the growth, prune them so that they are artificially dwarfed. This is high art that has been valued in Japan for years. Bontei is a closely related speciality. Origami – the art of paper folding – and Ikebana – the art of flower arranging – also have retro cool.

Swordsmith — Replica swords and scabbards are in demand by collectors and the sword and sorcery industry. The best are limited editions that are re-created to look and feel like the original medieval swords in every detail. Some are used in film projects such as *The Mask of Zorro*. A great sword maker will also be a great researcher, with a passion for the history of swords. This is a tiny niche so be prepared to look to America and countries such as Japan for mentors.

Taxidermist — The word taxidermy comes from the Latin taxis derma or arrangement of skin. Taxidermists were highly popular a century or more ago, but museums and a few astute collectors still use them. Highly retro-cool, taxidermists need to have a detailed knowledge of anatomy combined with artistic ability. They preserve the skins of animals, fish and birds to re-create an animal for mounting or in a particular scene or pose.

Health/Organic Food Store Owner — Once all food was 'natural'. Now health is on the menu once again. The organic and health-food markets are high-growth markets in the UK and North America. To start your own business, you can either own a shop or provide a delivery box scheme. You'll need to learn product selection, community and online marketing and have skills in managing employees and customer service as well as a passion for nutrition.

In the know
Celebrity Starter Careers

Madeleine Albright, President Bill Clinton's secretary of state and now the head of her own global strategy consulting firm, learned how to negotiate tricky deals by selling underwear in a department store.

Pamela Anderson started out as a fitness instructor in Canada.

Cate Blanchett started her career doing commercials in Australia and was the original 'Tim Tam girl'.

Tony Blair was once an aspiring rock star in the band Ugly Rumours, before being called to the bar in 1976.

Brenda Blethyn was born in 1946 in Kent and started her career working at British Rail in the 1960s. She took courses at the Guildford School of Acting and became an actress in the theatre, joining the National Theatre Company in 1975.

3. Outside the Mainstream

Joining the other rats on the rat-run to the daily rat race is just not cool. In fact, it is the guarantee of a so-so or even downright uncool career.

Forget a mere thirty-five hour week stuck in the office. Many of us work far more than the standard nine to five. The British worker works the longest hours in Europe, lagging only just behind the USA. Back in the Victorian era, on average people in the UK worked 50 hours a week. Until relatively recently, those figures were declining, but now they are on the rise again. Many workers don't even take a proper lunch break.

So, how can you capture some cool outside the mainstream? If you hate structure, don't want to work inside every day, or just want a simpler or more fulfilling life, consider how you can choose a less stressful or time-consuming career. Think about changing a hobby into a job. Focus on careers with more day-to-day variety.

Or, if you are really brave, go the whole hog and downshift. You will join nearly two million others in Europe who have taken the same path and chosen a simple job with fewer hours but more satisfaction than their successful but dull office rat-race.

I don't want to wear a suit and tie ...

CLASSIC COOL

Gardener — A professional gardener plants, maintains and, to varying degrees designs, gardens. You will be expected to work in all weathers and have an expert knowledge of plants and how they fit into different conditions. You can work for yourself, a company or possibly a garden that is open to the public.

Taxi Driver — A black cab driver in London has to pass a rigorous test of his familiarity of the city, known as the Knowledge. Other cities are less strict about qualifications, but you will need to be licensed. Drivers often own their own cars and are free to work flexible hours. You meet a lot of interesting people, but be aware that it can be a dangerous business: cabbies can get attacked by drunks, or robbed. If you are interested in the business side, however, you might even have the opportunity to build up a fleet of cabs.

Art Director — Art directors work on films and TV productions to make sure that the 'look' of the production is right. They may create sets, objects or scenery. They need to be good at drawing by hand or working on a computer. They are in charge of staff so will have to cope with budgets and oversee staff within the art department for the production.

Model Maker — You are more likely to be wearing protective clothing in this profession than a suit. Based in an office or studio, you will work with chemicals and materials such as fibreglass and resin to create 3-D images and models for architectural needs or museums, or props and figures for TV and film. You need a knowledge of maths, technical drawings and computer design.

VERY COOL

Photojournalist — Photojournalists work anywhere around the world. They are employed by newspapers and magazines to take pictures of subjects for articles for the print media. Their pictures are used to illustrate a newsworthy subject.

Wild Animal Trainer — Wild animal trainers train and care for animals in zoos. They act as animal keepers, looking after the animals and their diet, and may also perform in shows with the animals and the public. There are very few of these jobs, especially nowadays, and it helps to have a background in general animal behaviour, behavioural psychology, and possibly education. If you work with marine animals you will need to be physically fit and able to swim. On-the-job training is usually given.

Thatcher — Thatchers replace old thatched roofs and make new thatched roofs using coverings such as reed and long straw. You need to be physically fit so you can climb scaffolding and carry heavy materials. You must, of course, be prepared to work outdoors. You can train with a thatcher or, if you are under 25, with the Countryside Agency. Experienced thatchers can earn good money – but expect to start on less than £10,000.

Beekeeper — Most beekeepers in the UK are self-employed and few are full-time. To make money you will need to sell and market honey and have at least a hundred beehives. In the winter, beekeepers process the honey and in the summer they work outdoors collecting the honey and checking on the bee colonies. Contact beekeeping associations for more information.

Hot-air Balloon Crew — Crews manage balloons for one-off flights or hot-air ballooning holidays. These are sold in the UK, in Europe and in more exotic locations such as Africa (for balloon safaris). Crewmembers usually work as part of a team, inflating, deflating and crewing balloons for tourists. Map and compass skills are a necessity. The work is often available in overseas resorts so languages may be helpful.

Fine Artist — Many artists can't produce a regular income through art alone. However, they may take their art skills to areas such as animation, cartoons, book illustration or multimedia design. If you are going to make a career as a straight artist, make sure you are a good promoter of your own talents.

DJ — A DJing career can bring you money and stardom, if you have the talent and the drive. You can develop your own niche and play to your audience and get paid for it. There are some overheads, equipment and marketing, but your time is your own, and you don't have to wear a tie unless you want to.

✱ *UNUSUALLY COOL*

Honey-trap Woman –
'Honey-Trap Women' catch cheating men for a living. They work for private detectives, who are engaged to expose men for being unfaithful to their partners. They are given a photograph of the 'target' and wait for them

at a bar or restaurant. If the man takes the bait, the honey-trap woman will tape conversations as evidence to catch the man cheating. It's a career that could pay off too. You could get paid up to £200 per client.

Waxwork Maker –
Madame Tussaud started her business when she took plaster casts of French aristocrats during the French revolution. Nowadays the subject is more likely to be a footballer, politician or pop star, but there is still a call for waxwork making. Recently, the new Eastern European rich have been buying figures of themselves as artworks to keep at home.

I want every day to be a little different

CLASSIC COOL

Computer Games Designer — Top games designers need to combine technical skills with an up-to-date knowledge and passion for the games market. You are likely to work with a team of graphic artists and programmers, managing everything from script to animation, and using storyboards to present your ideas within a socialised company. It is a very competitive, profitable, growth, global industry, and creativity is often a better qualification than a particular degree. Linked careers are **Multimedia Designer** and **Website Developer.**

Corporate Video-maker — A corporate film-maker works for companies who want to promote their business to clients or keep their employees informed about the company's progress. Corporate communications, commercials and internet films are big business. You can work for yourself or a production house. You will need camera, casting and direction skills and the ability to understand the needs of a big corporation.

Literary Agent — Agents are mostly based in London and either work for agencies, in partnership or are self-employed. They promote author's works to publishers, film and TV. Agents need to be supportive of the talent they are promoting, and assertive enough to agree profitable deals and agree contracts and rights. Many specialise in a particular area, such as sport, travel, crime fiction or children's books. It is a very competitive area and agents are paid a commission of up to 15 per cent of their authors' earnings.

Small Business or Franchise Owner — If you own your own business, you'll be amazed at the skills you will pick up and how many different tasks you will need to learn. You may have to be your own marketer, accountant, salesperson, manager and strategist. If you are successful, you'll work long days, but unpredictable ones. A small business owner needs to be both a planner and a firefighter, ready to respond to every opportunity.

Bed and Breakfast Owner — The ultimate small business is in your own home where your customers literally come to you. Instead of your daily commute, you can walk to your own kitchen to prepare meals for your guests. Of course there are early hours, you need to have great entertainment skills and be good at fixing things. Also be prepared to sell and market yourself.

Resort Entertainer — If you have singing, dancing or circus skills, perhaps juggling or stilt walking, you could work for a resort as an entertainer. The Disney group is a big employer of parade entertainers, bringing characters to life for the tourists.

Location Scout/Manager — A location scout looks for locations to fit the script of a film or TV programme for a media production company or advertising agency. They need to find a suitable location and to work out the logistics of how to operate there. The location manager is the higher position. They deal with the rest of the production team after the location has been scouted to deal with any logistical problems that may arise. Like other media careers, you will have to prove your enthusiasm to a production company. A car is also useful.

VERY COOL

War Correspondent — Some journalists and broadcast journalists will become experienced in working in difficult areas of the world and eventually become war correspondents. Obviously, if you have had military or naval training it will help you to have this career, but it is not a necessity. This is not an entry-level profession but, if you are cool headed and really want it, enter journalism in the normal way and be ready to volunteer for the tough assignments.

Overland Expedition Leader — Overland expedition leaders drive and guide groups to interesting and remote areas of exotic countries. Mechanical knowledge is useful. You will need to be active, good-humoured, resourceful and well travelled, as well as being a good leader. It may also help to have languages or specialist knowledge. A similar career is a **Biking/Trekking Leader**. This career will also take you to some of the most interesting parts of the world, working outdoors, running holidays and designing trails.

Animal Actor Trainer — Animal actor trainers rear and train animals. They need to be able to provide a healthy environment for the animals to live in as well as to develop a business with all the marketing required. If you want to become an animal actor trainer, you may choose to specialise in a particular species of animal, e.g. dogs, cats or birds. Most animal training careers will need you to develop your own business, though you might be lucky enough to find a business that will train you up. It will be helpful to have some background in animal behaviour and behavioural psychology, and even theatrical experience.

Food Stylist — A food stylist or food dresser chooses and arranges food so it looks at its best for advertisements or magazine articles. Such beautifully arranged food isn't always perfectly natural, though. A food stylist may use special effects and tricks of the trade; hairspray and paint are useful, as is using a substitute food to look like another. Certainly don't assume you can eat the leftovers!

✱ *UNUSUALLY COOL*

Whale- or Dolphin-watching Guide –
Working (mainly) overseas, you will take out groups of tourists on tours in areas such as Mexico or Hawaii. Every day is different, simply because there is no way to predict where whales or dolphins can be found. Of course you will need good boat-handling and people skills.

Bison Rancher –

Farming is a classically unpredictable profession. Every day is guaranteed to be a little bit different. For the unusual, try cattle ranching, and, for the top of the unusual, take a look at bison. For a career where you cover hundreds of acres, bison ranching in the heart of the American countryside is hard to beat. You will be in charge of a head of several hundred bison used for meat processing and leather goods. You need to understand pasture and animal management. Naturally, the best place to learn is on the job.

Concert Promoter –

A concert promoter hangs with the band and gets to see the show but also does the hard work promoting the show. You will need to build up great contacts both with venues and bands. There are very few female concert promoters out there but many female stars, so there is potential for a good niche. You need to make your own market and you can earn either millions or negative numbers. It is up to you.

Ten tips for building a career outside the rat race ...

1. **Start your own business.**
   No longer will you have to call another person boss, or abide by the rules of others.

2. **Realise that technology is your friend.**
   It can liberate you from a daily commute and being tied to a desk.

3. **Get creative.**
   What do you really love doing? Find a career that is so cool it feels like you are playing rather than working. If you would do this career for free, it's probably a really cool career.

4. **Think in terms of supplying value rather than time.**
   People really want to buy results. They don't care how long you have spent working at something if it gives them the result they want.

5. **Re-think your time.**
   If you are self-employed and focusing on value not time, you don't have to work any hours you don't have to. You can work in the middle of the night, or the middle of the day. You can work five hours, or twenty-four, it's up to you.

6. **Build passive income.**
   Create income while you sleep, so you are earning 24 hours a day. A website is an ideal example of this.

7. **Build yourself a support system if you are working alone.**
   Everyone needs a helping hand. Remember you can network online or through your hobbies or profession.

8. **Learn some business set-up basics.**
   Create systems for things such as bookkeeping/tax rules. If you are not a detail person, don't worry, once is enough. Basic filing and record keeping should suffice after that.

9. **Not every business takes money to set up.**
   If you do a web-based business, domain names and web hosting are cheap. The next investment is your creativity, not your money.

10. **Think about what you like to have supplied to you in terms of results.**
    There are millions of people out there who could have similar wants. If you can give them what they want, you can earn money from what you supply.

4. Adrenalin Charged

Are you laid back, unambitious, relaxed to a fault? Or perhaps you are a driven personality – ambitious, go-getting and longing to live on the nail-biting edge of life? Why snore when you could soar?

I am driven and ambitious

A burst of adrenalin every day can produce a very cool career. Perhaps business is your forte? Are you an initiator of projects? Do you often find yourself in a leader position? Do you like to have status and the power to take the important decisions?

Are you a go-getter? Do you like an adrenalin rush, quick results and a buzz from your life? Is it natural for you to take charge? If so, these could be the careers for you.

CLASSIC COOL

Commissioning Editor — This is a competitive career. Commissioning editors decide what books and other publications a publisher will take on. They work as part of a team and need to be good with deadlines and tasks. Much of their time is taken up with meeting agents and authors. Generally, an editor has started in publishing as an editorial assistant before working their way up the ladder.

Auctioneer — An auctioneer sets up the auction, prices the goods and controls the sale. They know the local market and can stay in charge of the auction audience. They are also up to date with the business side of the auction, which includes commissions and sales laws.

News Bureau Chief — A bureau chief is the person in charge of a foreign office for a news organisation. They either work for national newspapers or for press syndicates. Their job is to gather stories and dispatch them to the head office. They are likely to be in charge of local reporters and translators.

Theatre Director — Theatre directors direct a cast of actors, singers and dancers, as well as the technical staff in charge of lighting, scenery and costume. They are in charge of interpreting the play to produce a new vision for the cast and audience. Some work primarily for one theatre; others may travel extensively, and work in repertory or local theatres.

News Editor — A news editor works for a newspaper. He or she is the person who decides what stories should be where in the next day's edition, and whose vision decides what news will be set out as the important stories of the day. They put together dummy layouts, and sometimes write headlines.

Programme Director — A programme director sets the schedule for a radio station or television channel. They will select programmes and have a budget to buy in programming from independent production houses or overseas. They need to understand their audience demographic, what will attract the most advertising revenue, and what the competition is running.

Story Editor — A story editor is in charge of a group of TV or film scriptwriters. For example, a long-running soap opera will employ a story editor to develop a story and hire in writers to build a script. They will then edit and supervise the scripts that are produced.

Foreign Correspondent — A foreign correspondent is a journalist working either for a newspaper or a broadcaster. They are based in, or travel to, different areas of the world. They may well speak the local language. They spot and file stories and need to move faster than their competitors.

City Trader — This is a job for which you will usually need to start young. It requires sharp reflexes and a good instinct. You will trade equities (shares), bonds, or futures and options. For more cachet, become a **Credit Derivatives Trader**. Credit derivatives is a new market that has developed over the last few years. Without going too much into the technicalities, you trade insurance against the risk of a bond going bust. You buy a bond and a swap. If the company that issued the bond goes bust, you still get your money back. Don't worry if you don't know what that means, the money that accompanies this career will soon give you the incentive to learn the details.

Human Rights Barrister — A classic aspirational career. Barristers are advocates who present cases in court; they may specialise in criminal or civil cases. Most barristers work from chambers and are self-employed. As masters of the law they are well rewarded. You can easily earn over £100,000 in this career. At the coolest end of the profession as a Queen's Counsel (QC), you could earn £500,000+ per year. Currently cool at the moment is the **Human Rights Barrister** (N.B. If you have the interest but lack the legal ability, you could take a look at other human rights careers).

Lobbyist/Public Affairs Consultant — Public affairs consultants are employed either by a consultancy or an organisation, such as a charity, pressure group, or professional association, or even an overseas government. Sometimes consultancies are part of a larger public relations (PR) company. By understanding how the political system works, they are able to offer advice to clients. A lobbyist could be paid anything up to £100,000, or more. Political lobbying consultancies are often located in London or Brussels.

Investment Banker (corporate finance) — Corporate financiers advise companies, institutions and governments on financial opportunities such as mergers and acquisitions, how to raise money, government privatisations, Initial Public Offerings (IPOs), management buyouts and flotations. You'll need to be a good researcher and financial modeller. For this, expect to be rewarded well. With experience, you could be earning up to £150,000 a year. The majority of investment bankers work for global companies and have the chance to work overseas.

* UNUSUALLY COOL

Mountie –
The Mounties, or Royal Canadian Mounted Police, are internationally recognised as one of the coolest of all police careers. Sadly you will have to be, or become, a Canadian citizen to be a Mountie. If you've got the right passport under your belt, though, all you need to do is to pass police aptitude tests and enrol as a cadet. Check out Canadian careers services for more details.

Astronaut –
Space is the final frontier for the ambitious. There are two types of astronaut: flight engineers or pilots fly the shuttle and may carry out experiments on board; researchers or mission specialists are the astronauts who perform spacewalks. They conduct the majority of the scientific experiments. Most astronauts are in their mid-30s. They have to be fit and scientifically educated. A degree in physics, medicine, aerospace engineering or electrical engineering is best. With increased co-operation among the space-going nations of America, Russia, China and Europe, languages are useful.

Paparazzo/celebrity photographer –
The professional photographer is always on-call. They are up to date on which celebrities will sell most magazines and they are prepared to camp out for hours or days to get the top picture. Most recently we have the seen the rise of the videorazzo – taking moving clips of the stars.

Four top tips for future leaders

The world is full of people who like being the leader. They enjoy supervising employees, giving orders, being the person who makes the final decision on a project and the one who gets tangible results. How do you know if you have it in you to head for the top?

1. **Know what will suit you.** Are you the next Donald Trump or Richard Branson? Would you prefer to climb up the corporate ladder of an established institution or build your own? Many 'in charge' careers are in traditional industries. But what about self-employment? Or would you prefer to be in charge within a creative industry?

2. **Focus on your strengths and talents.** Are you a strong decision maker? Are you able to take personal responsibility for decisions that affect other people's lives? Do you enjoy meeting people who have power and position?

3. **Define your ambitions.** Would you like to have power, responsibility or status? How good are your achievements so far? Perhaps you have already been elected to a position of responsibility, or won an award for a result that you have achieved.

4. **Consider your interests.** Looking at your hobbies and interests may give you an indication as to whether or not you would enjoy this type of

professional responsibility. In all industries, leaders are confident, sociable, assertive, prepared to take measured risks in following a vision, and optimistic and persuasive enough to bring others on board. Leaders in business and professional fields are generally well-informed about current affairs and politics. They enjoy keeping up with the trends in the economy and stockmarkets, and they may be natural salespeople or charismatic presenters.

If you are a leader rather than a follower, consider traditional careers in business, finance, consulting and other professional fields for a route to a cool career.

I want a life on the edge

Dangerous, fast-paced, exciting, adrenalin-charged. If any of these descriptions are hitting the right spot for you, then there are jobs aplenty waiting to open the gates to an exciting life. Working in Britain or overseas, on-shore or off-shore, what are the cool careers that take you to an exciting, fast action life on the edge? In fact, all these careers are very cool.

VERY COOL

Demolition Expert — Demolition is a way of taking down a defunct building or factory. You will have to learn how to work with explosives safely as it only takes seconds for a skyscraper to be destroyed. Demolition experts blow up structures using explosive technology, cranes, diggers, cutting torches and other equipment. The military use demolition experts, as does the solid propulsion industry. Shockwave physics and engineering mechanics will give you the right background for the most skilled areas of this work.

Mountain Rescue — In the walking and skiing seasons, some of the most beautiful places in the world are also the most dangerous, with the threat of bad weather and avalanches. Rescuers fly in by helicopter ambulance to save those who have become stuck. You will need medical skills for this career.

Bodyguard — Being a bodyguard is not all James Bond and getting shot – a lot of the time you'll be running errands or driving your client around. Most jobs are with rich businessmen, though celebrities and politicians also need bodyguards. It helps if you have trained in martial arts, as a soldier or police officer, or have worked in the secret services. If you are feeling very adventurous and want a large slice of danger, South America is where your pulse will really race. The International Bodyguard Association is the place for more general information.

Jockey — Being a jockey is a competitive career. If you have the skill and build to be a jockey, you can enter your sport via an apprenticeship. It's not a long career. Most jockeys will be retired by the time they are in their 40s. It's a demanding job but can lead to other related careers.

Tank Firefighter — Being a firefighter is always cool but, for an even cooler job, how about being a tank or oil well firefighter. The most famous blowout fighter was the Texan, Red Adair, who inspired a John Wayne movie. When Saddam Hussein set the Kuwaiti fields alight, $60 billion worth of oil was destroyed before 732 oil wells could be rescued. A crew can be called up at any time, earning a fee of between $20,000 and $200,000 to control a blowout. The members of the crew make about $300 to $1,000 a day. You'll need a drilling background and must be willing to travel a lot.

Smoke Jumper — Smoke jumpers are firefighters who parachute into remote areas to fight fires. They are airlifted into raging fires at low altitude – as low as about 450 metres (around 1,500 feet) – to backburn areas and stop fires. It requires endurance, strength and the ability to work without sleep. Clearly there's not much need in the UK. America might be the place for this career. Also check out **Bush Firefighters** in Australia.

De-miner/Minesweeper — Landmines or unexploded ordnance, also known as UXO, are a problem in many recovering war zones throughout the world. De-mining is a big industry in countries in Asia and Africa. Mine clearance personnel are former explosives and munitions experts who work for one of the twenty or so companies in this area. Money varies enormously, and the risk of being blown up is ever-present. If you like the sound of this career, take a look too at the police, who use bomb experts – though this is a highly skilled and competitive area.

Professional Hunter — Professional hunters work in different countries, including America and parts of Africa, hunting big game. They take groups or individuals on hunts, tracking animals such as elk and deer. You may need to learn calling and stalking techniques, horsemanship, orienteering and wilderness survival.

Explorer — Sir Ranulph Fiennes, Bear Grylls, Benedict Allen – these are some of the personalities who have made their name as explorers. Some prefer to scale mountains; others go in search of little-visited tribes. They raise money through sponsorship and writing books and articles.

* *UNUSUALLY COOL*

Bounty Hunter –

In the States, there are about 2,000 bounty hunters hunting down fugitives. It is estimated that, of the over 30,000 accused who jump bail, nearly 90 per cent are brought in by bounty hunters. They earn up to 30 per cent of the fugitives' bail from bail bondsmen. It doesn't require much training and you are not allowed to use a gun, so martial arts training wouldn't go amiss. Contact the National Institute of Bail Enforcement (America) for more information.

War Zone Engineer –

Where there is a war, there is usually a shattered economy and, a few years later, money to be spent from international organisations on infrastructure repair. If you prefer a slide rule to a gun, you can still go to adventurous places but, when you arrive, you'll be repairing pipelines or equipping towns with sewerage. You will be helping thousands of people get their lives back to normal.

COOL OR NOT SO COOL?

Terrorist Bounty Hunter — So far above the top rung of the unusually cool part of the coolometer that it may not be cool at all, is the terrorist bounty hunter. If you fancy travelling around the more remote parts of the globe, and speak good Arabic, French or local dialects, there is a job for you. But you could get shot. If you haven't been trained to a high level in the army, don't even go there.

Mercenary — Cleaning up the mess left by ongoing wars in remote regions – 'outsourcing military needs' is a big business. It attracts ex-soldiers (especially the SAS), and some companies provide training, equipment, humanitarian assistance, military contractual support, and democracy transition assistance programmes for the military forces of emerging republics.

20 surprisingly dangerous careers

If you would rather avoid danger in your career, it isn't always the obvious jobs that are the dangerous ones. According to research in America, some careers lay you open to unforeseen risks. Let's take physical attacks, for example. When you do a job where cash is visible, such as working in a convenience store or restaurant, you lay yourself open to robbery and violence. You also face similar risks working as a security guard or as a taxi driver. Fatal accidents from falls are high in the constructions industry, farm work, agriculture, forestry and mining. Recorded accidents include electrocutions, machines, trees and pipes turning into lethal missiles and hitting workers, as well as workers falling from scaffolding and ladders.

According to Oxford University researchers, the most dangerous jobs in Britain include fishing and the merchant navy. The safest jobs are in the service sector, with, pharmacists and insurance brokers being some of the safest careers, according to the insurance industry. One of the most dangerous jobs of all is as a window cleaner. After all, it's like performing in a circus with no net to catch you. Note that many of these jobs aren't paid in line with the level of danger, either.

1. **Retail sales person**
   Especially if you work in a convenience store.

2. **Journalist**
   If you are out and about, especially overseas, you expose yourself to adventure, sometimes of an unwelcome sort.

3. **Delivery person**
   If you deliver pizza or fill vending machines, it appears you are at the whim of traffic accidents, robberies and assaults.

4. **Taxi driver**
   You never know who's going to turn up in the back of your cab.

5. Fishermen and seafarers

Not only do fishermen face the danger of the world's oceans, but they also risk being hit by their own tools – nets, winches, hoists and cages – as well as drownings, collisions and groundings. A worker at sea is up to 50 times more likely to die while working than other workers.

6. Hospital nurse

Violence against nurses is always a problem in hospitals. Assault is an ongoing issue for all staff, from doctors to hospital porters.

7. Bush pilot

Not helped by the risk of ending up injured in a remote area far away from immediate medical help.

8. Crop duster pilots and air taxi pilots

Taking off and landing are the most dangerous bits of any flight, so any job that involves doing lots of both is clearly a risk!

9. Circus performer

Whether you are flying through the air on a trapeze or balancing on a thin pole, life is bound to be a bit unsafe.

10. Elephant trainer

There's always that danger of being crushed by a very heavy animal! **Lion tamers** had better beware as well.

11. Motorbike courier

Among the most dangerous of all jobs are those

of the motorbike couriers of Brazil but, even in
the average city, you could get injured.

12. **Construction worker/scaffolder/window
cleaner/structural iron and steel workers**
Anyone working on a high building is setting
themselves up for a dangerous career.

13. **Tree surgeon** or **logger**
Similarly, hanging off a tall tree isn't the safest of
professions.

14. **Police officer, traffic wardens** and **parking
attendants**
If you are dealing with the public, you might well
get hurt at some point.

15. **Teachers**
Unfortunately, hiding out in a classroom isn't
going to help either.

16. **Lorry driver**
All that time on the road exposes you to accident
risk.

17. **Bailiff**
If you try to take someone's possessions, they
don't like it.

18. **Electrical power line installers/repairers**
Even with safety precautions it can be
dangerous.

19. **Railway staff**
Once again, the public aren't always well
behaved.

20. Rubbish and recyclable material collectors
You could get cut on an unexpected object, or maybe it's all the hopping on and off a moving lorry.

In the know
Celebrity Starter Careers

Richard Branson dropped out of boarding school aged 16 to focus on his *Student* magazine. Although this was not a huge success, he began his Virgin mail order business aged 20 and rapidly expanded it into a music publishing business, a record company and record shops.

Derren Brown, the mentalist and illusionist, was born in Surrey and studied law and German at the University of Bristol. He worked initially as a conjurer and started performing stage hypnosis shows in the 1990s before studying NLP (Neuro-Linguistic Programming) and mind-reading.

Gordon Brown studied history at Edinburgh University and then stayed on to complete a doctorate. He was elected rector of the university before working as a journalist at Scottish Television.

Sandra Bullock was once a bartender before becoming an actress.

5. People love

Some of the coolest people in history have plumbed the depths of the human psyche to help us to understand what makes people tick, or they have led careers that have changed the lives of millions.

And don't dismiss those who make us look or feel better, either. Where would we be without the inventors of make-up, or gym equipment?

I like to understand people and know what makes them tick

Psychology and psychiatry are the conventional first ports of call for anybody who wants to understand what goes on inside another human being's head. However, there are also cool careers in the arts and entertainment industries that lead to deep levels of understanding about our fellow human beings.

And, if you want to get up close with the darker, shadowy side of humanity we would rather not always show the rest of the world, why not opt for a life of crime (on the side of the good guys, of course)?

15 places to find a people career

1. Physical and mental health care

2. Education

3. Therapy

4. Alternative therapy

5. Facilitation

6. Sales and persuasion

7. Counselling

8. Social work

9. Outplacement

10. Mediation

11. Conflict resolution

12. Religious and pastoral care

13. Rehabilitation

14. Community welfare

15. Childcare

MENTAL COOL

Experimental Psychologist — Experimental psychologists study human (and animal) behaviour, using data and scientific experiments in laboratories as academics, and also researchers, in a diverse range of industries from zoos to manufacturing and retail. They are interested in a wide range of psychological areas, including comparing species, understanding cognition, learning and conditioning, and the environment and its impact.

Hostage Negotiator — A hostage negotiator can train though a course with a law enforcement agency and will have a background in the police, military or special services. Training will probably be a succession of courses, as well as practical experience of crisis situations. You need to be a good listener and a skilled communicator with a strong understanding of psychology. In a negotiation situation, a negotiator must find out who the hostage taker is, what they want, and what can be done to resolve the situation, while avoiding harm to the hostages and bystanders.

Hostage/Cult Debriefer — Debriefing is a technique used after kidnappings and hostage takings, and related areas such as cult membership. The army, secret services and some specialist organisations employ professional psychologists, medics and post-traumatic stress disorder (PTSD) specialists skilled in this area to debrief individuals after traumatic events to help them deal with the stress.

Sports Psychologist — Athletes benefit from learning how to motivate themselves effectively for a competition, deal with anxiety, or the fear of failure. Sports psychologists may be employed to help individuals or teams. **Sports Coaches** also use some of these skills.

Neuropsychologist — A Neuropsychologist studies the way brain functions affect behaviour and feelings. How does your brain store memories? What happens when your brain is injured? **Clinical Neuropsychologists** assess and treat brain-injured people.

(Comic) Impersonator — An impersonator gets under the skin of a character and acts them out to an audience. Think Rory Bremner, Ronni Ancona or Alastair McGowan. Impersonators entertain audiences in clubs, on radio and TV, working by themselves or as part of an ensemble. They may find work through a talent or entertainment agent or directly.

VERY COOL

Playwright — As a playwright you will combine an understanding of the technicalities of writing dialogue and structuring a script with an understanding of different characters and their motivations. You may sell your script to a publisher, radio, TV or film company, or write for a particular theatre group. Many playwrights are freelance. You may engage an agent to act on your behalf.

Screenwriter — A screenwriter writes scripts for radio, television and film. Like a playwright, you need an understanding of the technicalities of writing and language as well as an understanding of people and the dynamics of how they interact. You may either write original work or adapt the work of other writers. Many scriptwriters are freelance, though major film studios employ regular writers, some of whom work in writers' groups. Another outlet for screenwriters is corporate video companies.

Crime Writer — Think of a crime writer such as Ruth Rendell or Ian Rankin. Many of the best-known characters from English literature have sprung from the pages of crime novels and this is a genre the British are particularly good at. An understanding of what motivates a killer and what happens when someone becomes a suspect is vital to become a good writer. A great crime writer also understands his/her audience, how to titillate and tease us, and how to make us believe the red herring is a real lead. Crime writers are freelance but may employ literary agents to sell their work.

Comic Character Actor — Use Al Murray the Pub Landlord, Alan Partridge, Dame Edna Everage, Ali G or Borat as a reference point for this job. This job is a combination of actor, comedian and impersonator, with a fine ability to work the audience. Hone a character and keep the same character in different contexts to provide entertainment on the club circuit, on radio or TV.

NLP Practitioner — NLP – Neuro-Linguistic Programming – is the study of people, change and results. How can you change someone's unconscious thinking to help them therapeutically or in business? Studying NLP is well structured and many NLP graduates apply their skills to coaching, sales or training. You can also become a certified trainer of NLP if you want to teach others.

Mentalist — Derren Brown is the role model for a successful mentalist. He combines stage magic and Neuro-Linguistic Programming to motivate people to behave differently through his understanding of the unconscious mind. If you are interested in becoming a mentalist you might want to train as a **Stage Magician** or **Stage Hypnotist**.

I want to help people change their lives

If you are kind and caring and want to help others change their lives for the better, you'll need to be *genuinely* interested in other people, otherwise your job will begin to pall in an instant. Keep an eye out for possibilities either working with individuals or groups to help people to overcome mental, emotional or physical problems, or perhaps become productive members of society.

For the most unusual careers, hunt down new careers in the alternative self-help and mind body spirit industries. They are high growth and high niche.

CLASSIC COOL

Occupational Therapist — If you want to help people with physical or psychological problems, this could be the career for you. You will need to be a good listener and be able to get your clients to trust you enough that they can open up to you. Occupational therapists may have to deal with the victims of accidents or depression, and it will be up to you to help your clients to cope, learn physical activities, or get around the home after an accident.

Religious Worker — Religious workers such as Catholic priests, rabbis, and Church of England clergy combine spiritual teaching and understanding with a focus on the needs of the groups of people they serve. They conduct religious rites, write sermons, conduct marriages and funerals, and comfort the sick.

Clinical Psychologist — A clinical psychologist deals with mental, emotional and behavioural issues – from clinical depression to phobias or schizophrenia. They may work with doctors or specialise in a particular area, such as with the problems of the elderly or the young.

Occupational and Organisational Psychologists — These psychologists are particularly interested in how people function in the workplace. Some work in human resources within companies, in employee development and assessment, training and coaching. Others work in a more strategic management consultant role, advising on planning for culture, staffing or organisational change projects. **Career Consultants** advise on career *choices* for individuals; **Outplacement Consultants** advise on career *changes*.

VERY COOL

Animal Therapist — Animal therapists instruct adults and children in animal care and welfare issues. At the same time they may visit institutions, such as schools and nursing homes, with therapy dogs or other animals to share the therapeutic experience of being around animals.

Music Therapist — It has been intuitively known for centuries that music has a therapeutic effect on people with depression and even physical illness. The work a music therapist can do is highly varied. One day they might be helping a sufferer of Alzheimer's; the next they could be bringing music to cheer young cancer sufferers. They may use recorded music, sing or play a particular instrument. They work in hospitals, mental health care centres and in schools.

Art/Creative Therapist — Art and creative therapists work with children and adults who have special needs, such as behavioural problems or severe learning difficulties, providing programmes where the clients use art, crafts and sculpture for therapy. They may also work in rehabilitation programmes or in nursing homes. One of the ways to get into this area is through voluntary work.

Dance Therapist — Dance therapists use dance and other physical movements to help patients with their physical and mental health. They are employed in prisons, health and mental health care centres, as well as educational facilities. If this therapy appeals, take a look at Eurythmy, a Rudolf Steiner form of dance therapy that is used to restore harmony to the person.

✳ *UNUSUALLY COOL*

Divorce Hypnotherapist –
Therapy after divorce is a growing industry. After all, when divorce lawyers cost up to £500 an hour, it is cheaper to sort yourself out. While conventional services offered by charities like Relate are effective, hypnotherapy for divorcees, either one-to-one or in groups, is a new area. If you go down this route, study as a conventional hypnotherapist. You can also build your business for other problems such as self-esteem or weight loss. A more extreme, though related, career may involve past-life regression hypnotherapy.

EMDR Specialist –
Eye Movement Desensitisation and Reprocessing (EMDR) is a treatment technique invented in the 1980s and originally used to treat trauma survivors. It is now used with phobias and other problems. The therapist waves their fingers in a pattern in front of the client's eyes. The client tracks the movements while focussing on a traumatic event. Afterwards the client is able to feel calmer about the event. Most practitioners are self-employed.

Angel Therapist –
Angel and ascension teachers and therapists believe that they can call on angels to help people with issues in their lives. The author Doreen Virtue has written many books on angels, so many practitioners use to her work as a reference for understanding the subject.

Horse Whisperer –
Monty Roberts was the man who invented a method of training horses, based not on 'breaking' the horses but on communicating with them. You can train in his and similar methods in several countries including the UK. His methods are now used to help people feel better and change as well.

I love children

Looking after helpless infants is always cool. If you prefer children to adults, look no further.

KIDDIE COOL

Private Maternity Nurse — A relatively new phenomenon, private maternity nurses care for newborn babies in the home to help out stressed and tired parents. Most are experienced nannies, registered nurses, ex-midwives or health visitors. They deal with feeding, laundry and even cooking for the mother. They can earn between £125 and £200 a day and stay for two to eight weeks from the birth.

Child Carer — If you are looking after children you'll always have a different routine each day. Of course, you'll need lots of patience and be good at establishing strong boundaries, as well as being nurturing and caring. You can train as a nursery nurse through a full-time course, or on the job. There is a growing need for qualified careers and many now receive handsome perks. Be aware, it's a tiring career so it would be wise to try it out through playgroup or nursery work first.

Educational Psychologist — How do you motivate a student to learn? An educational psychologist wants to know how to make learning and teaching effective for the individual. **School psychologists** counsel students and assess the need for intervention in children with behavioural problems.

Birth Coach — Having an active birth is getting more fashionable. It is considered very uncool just to be knocked out by pain-relieving drugs like many mothers. How much cooler to have an empowered and relaxed birth where you are fully alert to what is going on. As a birth coach you might want to qualify in nutrition, pregnancy yoga, maternity care, hypnosis and other areas so that you can coach mothers to release their anxieties and fears around giving birth. Hypnobirthing is a related area.

Adoption Specialist — An adoption specialist provides services to the birth parents, adoptee and adoptive parents. They may advise on different routes for adoption and provide referrals and assessments of prospective adoption families. Some also carry out specialist search services overseas. An adoption specialist needs to be able to help families with the emotional side of the process as well as the rules and regulations.

* *UNUSUALLY COOL*

Parenting Coach –
For the last half a century or so there have been numerous authors advising parents on how to bring up their children. There have been various incarnations over the years, including Dr Spock and Gina Ford. In our time-pressed economy, the parenting coach can provide a service by writing books and advice columns, or by running workshops and coaching.

I want to make people look or feel better

Wanting to look good may be considered superficial by many people, but this comes into the cool category for a good reason – if you make people feel better by improving their looks, you will always have an appreciative client base and feel that you have chosen a pretty cool career.

However, if you want to have widespread recognition

from the rest of the world that what you are doing is as close as you can get to cool sainthood, why not help people heal. There will be a 'cool halo' over your whole career.

LOOKING COOL

Plastic/Cosmetic Surgeon — 'Plastics' is an increasingly common profession. It even has a lower entry point than in the past. You can now specialise in some procedures, such as Botox, with less medical training. But, if you want to be really cool, consider whether you are the right gender. There are surprisingly few female plastic surgeons around, and there is huge demand from female patients.

Personal Stylist/Style Consultant — For a career with much less training, a personal stylist styles a client's wardrobe by making a 'closet edit', taking clients shopping, evaluating their body shape and colour type and teaching them how to dress in their best style and colours. You may also want to write fashion articles. Many of the top stars have their own stylists. Some big stores also employ personal shoppers/advisers.

Fashion Stylist — A fashion stylist works in the fashion industry casting models for fashion shoots, choosing clothes, liaising with hair and make-up artists, coming up with a creative concepts and attending fashion shows. It's hard work, odd hours and highly competitive. Look to fashion magazines for a possible way in. A related career is as a **TV Wardrobe Stylist**.

Weight-loss Coach — A weight-loss coach may use a combination of nutrition and motivation techniques, such as Cognitive Behavioural Therapy, Neuro-Linguistic

Programming or hypnosis, to help people achieve their goals successfully. They usually run their own businesses and work with individuals one-to-one or through workshops. Hypnotherapy or nutrition is a good route into this career.

Lifestyle Guru — It's a loose term, but a lifestyle guru could do anything from help their clients choose their clothes to nutritional, spiritual, health or self-development advice. They might even organise their lives, helping them to find a place to live, employing staff or advising them on feng shui or etiquette. You will need to be a confident and charismatic person to have this career.

Laughter Yoga Teacher — Nothing makes people look better than a natural smile. Laughter yoga is a growing area across the world. Laughter yoga uses yoga breathing and relaxation techniques along with other exercises to induce laughter, tone muscles and to boost the immune system as well as to improve general health and fitness levels.

Happiness Trainer — This is a related career to laughter yoga, in which you research and teach individuals or groups ways to be actively happy. This is a very new area of research and you may also find references to the similar area of positive psychology.

Indian Face Rejuvenation Specialist — Indian face massage, along with acupuncture, is sold as a natural, non-invasive method of facelift that has been growing in popularity as people look for alternatives to plastic surgery. Also known as Indian Champissage, it is based on theories of massage and energy. Facial acupuncture for a youthful appearance requires full acupuncture expertise and is based around theories of balancing qi (energy) in the face.

✱ *UNUSUALLY COOL*

Facial Exercise Guru –
Eva Fraser is one of the best-known facial exercise specialists. Facial exercise experts teach how you can keep a toned, more youthful looking face naturally through a series of exercises – in the same way as you would tone your body through going to a gym. You can train in this method through classes or DVD.

FEELING COOL

Health Psychologist — How do psychological factors affect illness? Why are some people able to give up smoking and not others? How do you reduce obesity, substance abuse or teenage pregnancy levels nationally? In this career, you could work with a doctor or in a hospital, and educate other medical personnel or look at research to develop and implement a health-related strategy and programme affecting society.

Crystal Healer — Crystal healers claim to use different crystals to produce a therapeutic effect on the body. There are courses of up to two years where you can learn which crystals correspond to which healing effects. There are many other careers now developing in the area known as vibrational medicine.

Integrated Medical Doctor — Over the last decade there has been a move by some medical professionals to advise private clients on both Western and alternative (vibrational) medicines as part of a holistic approach to health. Dr Ali in London is one of the best-known UK practitioners.

Cranialsacral Therapist — Cranialsacral therapy is a very non-invasive hands-on method of working with the craniosacral system of the body – the system that surrounds and protects the brain and spinal chord. Therapists aim to help the patient's body to self-correct by using very gentle touching of the system. Often this therapy is used with other complementary therapies. The Metamorphic Technique is another non-invasive technique, which uses light touch along the spinal reflex points of the head, hands and feet. It can be used by babies or adults to make the person feel better.

Gong Master — Gong therapy is a form of sound healing. There are only a very few, but a growing number, of practitioners in the UK. Sound and music have been used for thousands of years for healing as well as for relaxation. The gong drum is an instrument that is said to produce the original sound of the universe – OM – when played. This is supposed to be the most harmonious sound we can hear and therefore restores us to balance. **Sound Therapists** use other instruments, such as singing bowls, tuning forks or even just the natural singing voice. As well as therapy in private groups for meditation, they may play in hospitals, care homes or prisons, at weddings, funerals or parties.

Kinesiologist — Kinesiology is the skill of muscle testing to diagnose and correct imbalances in the body. In kinesiology you learn to balance the acupuncture, lymphatic, vascular and emotional systems of the body. You can test for food intolerance and nutritional deficiencies in the body.

Tai Chi Chuan Teacher — Tai chi is the ancient Chinese physical and mental practice that has thousands of years of history behind it. It is notably good for keeping people flexible right up into their old age, and it is practised by millions of people in China. Now it is taught across the country. If you are enthusiastic about the principles behind this art, consider also learning the related Qi Gong, but both will take many years to master to teacher level.

Iridologist — Iridology has been around for centuries. Iridologists believe that they can detect changes in a person's health by examining the iris of the eye for changes of colour or markings. These are said to relate to specific conditions in the rest of the body, for example, disease in the liver or kidneys, heart or spleen.

Bodyworker — Bodywork describes healing through touch and the physical manipulation of the body. Massage is a form of bodywork, but bodywork specifically includes other touch and healing tools, as well as techniques for postural alignment. The term bodywork is now used to cover specific trainings that may include tools from myofascial release or chiropractic techniques.

✱ *UNUSUALLY COOL*

Magnotherapist -

Magnotherapy is the practice of using magnets for healing and controlling pain. It was used at least three thousand years ago in China, and is said to help the body to heal naturally by promoting blood flow, the growth of new cells, and by reducing lactic acid. Electromagnetic and static field magnotherapy are both used by practitioners who work in areas such as childbirth or physiotherapy, or help people with conditions such as arthritis, ME or insomnia. There are also more people who specialise simply in selling magnet products.

In the know
Celebrity Starter Careers

Warren Buffett is arguably the world's top investor. Now in his 70s, he chairs a long-term investment company with more than $2 billion in holdings. Brought up in Omaha, Nebraska, he played the stock market when he was only eleven and, at high school, he is said to have made $50 a week from a pinball business he ran with a friend – his profit bought him 40 acres of land. After graduating, he went on to business school and worked first for three years for his father's investment banking company and then as an analyst. He started his own company at 25.

David Cameron, the leader of the Conservative party, was a political researcher after graduation. After the 1992 election he became a special adviser to the Conservative government and then was the director of corporate affairs at Carlton Communications.

Mariah Carey sang in talent shows and music festivals, but made money sweeping up hair in a salon in Manhattan. She worked as a waitress in several restaurants and as a coat checker long before finding success with the sale of over six million copies of her 1990s debut album, *Vision of Love*.

Bill Clinton taught law at the University of Arkansas in the 1970s when he was in his 20s, before becoming the youngest governor in Arkansas history and, in 1992, president of the United States.

Courteney Cox is the youngest of a family of thirteen children and stepchildren from Alabama. She dropped out of college and, despite being only 5'5", was soon in demand as a model in teen magazines and commercials. She also worked as an assistant in a music agency. In 1984, she won a role as a Bruce Springsteen fan in the video of 'Dancing in the Dark'.

6. Saving the World

Do you want to make the world a better place? Do you love nature, the planet, its trees, its plants, its animals? If you want to do something meaningful with your life, finding a cool green career is very 21st century. While, only a decade ago, some of these careers would be thought very unusual, nowadays it is both relatively mainstream and very cool to be at one with nature.

I love the planet

Green careers are the new black – aspirational and very chic. If you want, you can go right back to nature or, if you prefer, you can 'do green' from the comfort of an office. Here is a selection of careers in which you can save the planet (or at least a small part of it).

NATURALLY COOL

Medical Herbalist — A medical herbalist uses traditional Western herbal medicine to treat a variety of health conditions. Some herbalists also campaign to promote the use of herbal medicine through workshops. There are many different traditions of herbalism from Western to Indian and Hawaiian. The Chinese often use natural herbs in conjunction with acupuncture.

Corporate Social Responsibility Expert — Corporate Social Responsibility (CSR) has grown from nothing over the last few years. More and more companies across the globe are looking not only at the profit they make, but also at how they impact communities and the environment. As a CSR expert you may advise or report on this area. You can enter the corporate world through a CSR or environmental speciality, or perhaps through public relations.

Environmental/Conservation Educator — Environmental educators work at a centre in an area such as a national park or within a large campaigning organisation. Their job is to raise the environmental awareness of youth groups and adults, and they may research areas such as conservation, waste, sustainability or pollution. Obvious routes to this career are via a related degree or having started off in the voluntary sector. Educators are also found in zoological parks and aquariums.

Agricultural/Environmnental Geneticist — Geneticists specialise in many areas, including plant genetic engineering and genome mapping in order to increase crop yields and increase resistance of crop strains to pests and extreme weather conditions. It is also now possible to use genetics to find out what pollutants are present in an environment by using 'bio-sensor' technology.

Animal Geneticists — Animal geneticists work in breeding projects to preserve species of animals that are in danger of extinction. This is a very cool career to have, but clearly requires a high level of academic ability and qualifications – at least a Master's degree and a background in genetics and molecular biology.

VERY COOL

Sustainable Product Designer — A sustainable product designer is trained as a designer in the normal fashion, but has an awareness of the impact of his or her product on the environment. A linked career, which is becoming more popular, is the design of eco-homes and sustainable buildings or, for a slightly more down-to-earth career, how about specialising in checks on environmental friendliness of residential or commercial buildings?

Eco-tourism Owner/Guide — There is more and more awareness of the impact of tourism on the local environments and communities to which tourists travel. Eco-tourism seeks to minimise that impact and also, on occasion, to bring benefits to the local communities. It is an asset to have a particular field of knowledge – a local language, or a botany or geology background, for example. Wilderness survival skills, sailing or first aid skills could also be beneficial.

Green Woodland Manager/Charcoal Producer — If you want to live in an eco-friendly way, this ancient craft is still available as a career if you want to educate others through workshops and demonstrations of the craft.

Eco-bike, Trike, Trailer or Kart Builder — Although there are many big companies in the world making professional bikes, there are a few individuals who make custom-made individual transportation using ecological materials.

* UNUSUALLY COOL

Carbon Trader –
London is now the hub of the world's fast-expanding
carbon-trading market – a market for trading carbon
emissions (within the Kyoto Protocol) – as part of
London's financial markets. Companies have been
given credits or allowances to emit a certain amount of
pollutants. If they want to exceed that amount they must
buy credits from others who don't want to use their
whole allowance. Traders control the transfer of these
credits. Governments also have personnel involved in
the regulation of the trading markets.

Biodynamic/Steiner Farmer –
Biodynamic farming is a spiritual, holistic and spiritual
form of farming practised according to the principles
described by the scientist Dr Rudolf Steiner in 1924.
Biodynamic farming works with 'life energies', with
the intention of producing pure and energy-laden food.
Crops are organic, and sowing and harvesting are
dependent on the influences of the moon and planets
and the type of environment. No chemicals are used in
crops, or hormones in animal husbandry. Produce is
reportedly high in nutrients and the farming does not
deplete the soil. For more information, you can contact
the Biodynamic Agricultural Association (BDAA), which
promotes knowledge of, and training in, biodynamic
farming

Permaculture Farmer –
Permaculture aims to create a farming system that
is economic and also ecologically sound and sustainable. It is based on traditional ways of living and

farming, but also uses modern scientific knowledge. The basic philosophy, like Steiner, encourages care for the earth and its people, and 'co-operation with nature'. Permaculture is being used in Central and South America, integrating the traditional farming practices of the indigenous peoples.

Ethnobiologist –

Ethnobiology sits between love for people and love for the planet. It is the study of how human societies relate to ecosystems, their environment and its plants and animals. It draws on other disciplines, such as anthropology, linguistics and biology. It is also referred to as biological anthropology. Most conventional ethnobiologists examine how indigenous societies use flora and fauna, including in plant medicines. Many ethnobiologists are academics who sometimes spend months at a time out in the field recording local knowledge for future generations.

I want to save the people of the world

Do you want to fight for the rights of others, save the practices of cultural groups from extinction, or make the policies that will bring people out of poverty? Perhaps you want to discover a vaccine that will help millions, invest in companies that do good in their communities, or stop terrorists or foreign powers who want to kill thousands? If so, choose a career that focuses on saving the people of the world.

CLASSIC COOL

Political Researcher — Politics is an obvious route for anyone who wants to help the people of the world. You can try to get elected as a local, European or national politician. If you want a non-elected route, why not begin your career as political researcher, writing reports on particular issues and campaigns, monitoring the press and assisting with constituency issues. You can look for employment with MPs, political parties, lobbying and pressure groups, or related careers can be found in the civil service, the European Union and academia.

VERY COOL

Socially Responsible Investor — A socially responsible investment manager or analyst invests in shares that are ethical on behalf of private clients or institutions. In other words, they take account of the people they impact and/or the environment. They may also manage other funds as well.

Geneticist — Perhaps you want to do something more hands-on to save the people of the world? Geneticists deal in genes – the working parts of DNA – that make up the human blueprint. Clinical/medical geneticists diagnose genetic conditions, examining abnormal chromosomes and checking the inheritance of disease and mutations. Geneticists can also find work in biomedicine – the Human Genome Project is seeking to sequence all the genes in the human genome to make it possible to locate genes that cause disease, and produce new drugs. You will need a postgraduate degree for advanced research work.

Human Rights Specialist — 'Human rights' may encompass ideas such as civil liberties, democracy and good governance. Human rights specialists work for governments, including for the Foreign Office in the UK. Human rights activists and campaigners work for a variety of charities such as Amnesty International and Liberty. Human rights lawyers advise on personal and international situations.

Women's Rights Expert/Campaigner — Within the human rights field, women's rights and women's studies is an interesting specialist area for campaigners and experts. You may cover ideas, such as gender discrimination and equality and poverty, reproductive rights and population issues. You might find employment in international organisations such as UNICEF, or in campaigning and voluntary organisations.

International Trade Negotiator — Trade negotiators work on behalf of the government of a country in negotiation, such as with the World Trade Association. In this area and the campaigning area of trade justice, a legal background sets a course to become a skilled negotiator.

Human Security Expert/Campaigner — Human security is a fairly new idea that is used to describe the protection of an individual or a community from political violence. Unlike national security, human security focuses on the threats to populations from many different factors, including civil war and displacement or genocide. Human security specialists are found in government, international charities and academia.

Social Enterprise Entrepreneur — Social enterprises are businesses that are set up with the purpose of fostering lasting social and environmental change. Examples include businesses such as The Big Issue, Jamie Oliver's Fifteen and The Co-operative Group. They are found across industries, from farmers' markets to football supporters' trusts. Since 2005, when there were over 55,000 social enterprises in the UK, they have been able to register as a Community Interest Company – a limited company set up for community benefit rather than for private profit. For more information check out *www.cicregulator.gov.uk*.

✶ *UNUSUALLY COOL*

Cult Buster –
How better to help people all over the world than to stand up against organisations that seek to take over our minds? A cult buster/deprogrammer or exit counsellor helps people to exit authoritarian religious organisations. They investigate suspected cults, whose leaders encourage their recruits to isolate themselves from friends and family or relinquish their critical thinking skills, and may also expect them to forfeit property.

Inner City Ghetto Teacher –
If you love danger, one place to find it is in a school in an inner city ghetto in a part of the world where life is poor and dangerous. While you will be doing something meaningful, the dangers are real. In America, for example, you will deal with the crime produced in poor and disadvantaged areas, including guns and drugs.

MI6 (SIS) –
What better way to look after people than to ensure their safety? The Secret Intelligence Service (SIS) is

the global secret service for the UK that collects secret foreign intelligence. It employs a range of skilled people, including linguists and experts in technology, as well as operational officers. You will need to be a British citizen, and at least one of your parents must be a British citizen or have substantial ties to the United Kingdom. You will also have to pass a medical and a security vetting process, including drugs testing. Contact www.siscareers.gov.uk for more information.

Animals are my best friends

Have you ever wondered how you could make animals the focus of your career? If you want to care for animals or work with animals, start by thinking about the type of animals you want to work with. Mammals or birds? Domestic animals, livestock, marine or exotic, or wild animals? Perhaps insects or fish are more your thing? Now think about the role you want to have. Are you a scientist who wants to observe behaviour? Do you want to educate or perhaps entertain? Conservation? Rehabilitation or rescue? Competition is very tough so make sure that you are passionate about the role you choose – you won't always be paid that well.

CLASSIC COOL

Animal Inspector — Animal inspectors need to be at least 22 before they can qualify. You can train in the work with the RSPCA, learning about relevant law, animal rescue, some veterinary training and animal handling. It is also important to be a driver and physically fit.

Dog Trainer — Do you want to be the next Barbara Woodhouse or Victoria Sitwell? A dog trainer may lead obedience classes or work one-to-one with dogs exhibiting difficult behaviour. You are likely to be self-employed or working in a dog shelter or day care centre, and obviously need to learn about canine behaviour. For linked careers, look at becoming a **Groomer, Breeder** or **Kennel Owner** (in the States, the name for this is pet hotelier). Your job is to give pets a holiday while their owners are on holiday.

VERY COOL

Animal Pathologist — This is a very specialised profession. Animal pathologists need to decide the cause of an animal's death. They work with vets and government departments and may be called to look at pets, livestock or zoo animals. Sometimes they are employed in pharmaceutical companies or as researchers. However, at the moment, there are only 100 or so in the UK. You will need to be a member of the Royal College of Pathologists with a veterinary degree.

Animal Phsyiotherapist — A human physiotherapist is a respectable enough career, but take an extra qualification and you could spend your time helping animals with their joint and muscular aches and pains. For high-value animals like racehorses, animal physiotherapists are more and more in demand.

Animal Behaviourist/Psychologist — If you really want to become friends with an animal, why not learn to see inside their mind? Animal psychologists help pets to stop inappropriate behaviour, such as being aggressive, biting, destroying their environment or using their homes as a toilet. You can work in a veterinary practice or kennel, or work freelance, but, at present, there is no standard route as the numbers employed are so small. However, a psychology, behavioural science or veterinary background is useful.

Animal Sanctuary Owner/Manager — If you want to make a profession of this you may need to have your own wealth, a job on the side, a rich uncle or great sales skills. Once the money part is solved, this is clearly an immensely satisfying career for anyone who loves animals. Take your choice: you can save hedgehogs in England or perhaps big cats in Africa.

Llama or Alpaca Farmer — Llamas and alpacas are bred for their soft wool. Alpacas are big business in the USA, where they can sell for up to $60,000. You can sell the wool or use it yourself to make items such as hats, scarves and socks. If you like the idea of breeding animals, take a look at **Deer** or **Goat Farming** or travel abroad to find more exotic industries.

Racehorse Trainer — There are only around 500 trainers in the UK, all of whom are granted a licence by the Jockey Club. Trainers usually need money to buy and run their own stables, in which they may train their own horses or train horses for other owners. You will need to have business and staff management skills as well as an understanding of breeding lines, stallions and broodmares. Being a jockey or assistant trainer is good preparation or this type of work.

If you want a related profession, how about becoming a **Horse Rescuer**, **Groom**, **Riding School Teacher**, **Stables Manager**, **Horse Breeder**, or **Show-jumper**? There are a quarter of a million people employed in the horse industry in the UK and about 100,000 in racing.

* *UNUSUALLY COOL*

Cattle Rancher –
If you are bored of being a city slicker, have good riding skills and yearn for thousands of open acres and mountain trails, take a trip to cowboy country in the USA. It is hard work for not much pay, but definitely cool.

I love exotic animals most of all

If you want a wild animal career think about your own flexibility. Are you looking for a career in your own country or is half the appeal the chance of working overseas in different environments? What cultures appeal to you? Are there any political issues to think about? Do you want to work with captive animals or wild animals? Do you want to work inside or outdoors? Once you have decided on the details, open yourself up to a career that most people will consider very cool indeed.

VERY COOL

Shark Keeper — This is not the obvious job for many people, with the film *Jaws* so associated with the reputation of this huge marine creature. However, this makes it a niche and very cool career. In fact, most sharks are harmless to humans. Looking after sharks in an aquarium is not dangerous, but is satisfying. The competition is huge, so you will need passion and a qualification in zoology or marine ecology, and a thirst for research. Contact The Shark Trust for more information.

Herpetologist — Reptiles can provide you with a great career. Think of Steve Irwin, who became a TV celebrity out of herpetology. You can, of course, be an animal keeper, or you can turn reptiles into a business through breeding snakes for sale or providing venom for the medical industry. If you want to be very specialist, think about breeding endangered species. Most careers do require a higher degree qualification in the subject.

Animal Nutritionist — Where wild animals are kept in zoos or in any kind of captivity, they have special dietary needs. It is difficult to replicate their natural diet through prepared food so nutritionists are needed to ensure the survival of the animals. Entry to this area could come through a degree in nutrition or veterinary medical science.

Aquaculture Specialist — Aquaculture produces marine animals for food. It is a growth industry because the global demand for quality of seafood is rising. You can train directly for the industry. You will need to have knowledge of specialist areas, such as water quality management and filtration.

Wildlife Biologist — A wildlife biologist researches animals in the field or in captivity. Similar careers are as a **Field Biologist** and **Research Biologist**. These are all careers that are very important in species survival.

Biologists help to develop conservation programmes and determine the best conditions for breeding. You will need a Master's degree in an area such as botany, the biological sciences or zoological research. Be warned, you may spend time living in very basic conditions in the field. Tracking ability could be a plus in some environments.

Wild Animal Trainer — Animal trainers put on shows for the public, as well as training animals in zoos and conservation parks. Being the animal's keeper is part of the job too, so you will need to be able to take care of food preparation and the animal's behaviour. Many people want this job. Competition is fierce. A degree in psychology or a biological field is probably a minimum. An ability to entertain and communicate with the public is also vital. For a similar role, consider becoming a **Circus Trainer.**

Wild Animal Behaviourist — A wild animal behaviourist interprets and corrects abnormal behaviour. You will need to conduct behavioural studies and understand factors, such as the effects of breeding and environment on animals, as well as having a deep knowledge of the natural history of animals. A Master's degree or higher in an area such as animal psychology or the biological sciences is an ideal entry point.

Curator of Collections — A curator is in charge of all animal records in a zoo or specialist breeding facility for wild animals. There are many different curator roles at zoos. The curator of collections will liaise with other countries on captive management programmes and deal at the highest levels on conservation issues. A biological science or similar degree is the minimum starting point into this career.

In the know
Celebrity Starter Careers

Johnny Depp was brought up in Florida and left school aged 15 to try his luck as a rock musician. He sang for a series of bands including The Kids, before making the transition into acting after a visit to California. He made his first appearance in the film *A Nightmare on Elm Street* in 1984.

Michael Dell, the founder of Dell Computers, began his company at the University of Texas. He invested a small amount of money in computer parts to upgrade some old PCs. He made so much profit in one month that he left university.

Danny Devito trained as a hair stylist before making his break as a comic sitcom actor.

7. Sense-able

Creativity always passes the cool test. Not everyone is equally creative, but creative people impact on us everyday. Could you be one of them? Do you have a finely tuned sense of taste, a particular skill for sound? Perhaps you can create something of beauty from nothing.

Our mental image of a creative person tends to be of the struggling artist or sculptor, often working by him or herself for little or no money. That's not the truth in the 21st century. While some creative types may stick to the old career formats, there are plenty of cool careers for creative, big-picture thinkers with the ability to use their drive, ideas and intuition to get projects started and to see links, possibilities and opportunities where uncreative people see nothing. Here are some of the coolest careers for people who want to use taste, touch, sight and smell as the basis for a cool career.

Sound strikes a chord with me

Singing or playing an instrument are the obvious ways to get into a sound-based career, but which direction should you turn if you don't think you are a future Pavarotti, Robbie Williams or Shirley Bassey? You will need some talent to take up any sound-based career. Here are a few to start you thinking.

CLASSIC COOL

Composer — A composer writes music from scratch. Their music may be used in the theatre, for opera, musicals, film, TV or as a performance piece. Andrew Lloyd Webber is an example of a popular composer who has made a lot of money from his creativity. Many pop and rock artists are also original composers, as well as singers and lyricists.

Singing Telegram — A singing telegram messenger delivers a birthday, hen or stag party message to a recipient. Generally they are dressed in a particular costume that may or may not be sexually provocative, depending on the service. They may also play an instrument while they sing the message.

Lyricist — A lyricist is primarily a wordsmith, but one with enough sense of sound and rhythm to be able to fit their words to a melody generally written by someone else. They may work in partnership with a composer, or work for a performing artist or a commercial record or advertising company. A similar career is that of the **Jingle Writer.**

Sound Effects Technician — Sound effects specialists are needed to produce the sound effects that accompany the broadcast of a television or radio production. They choose sounds that add emotion or atmosphere to a sequence.

Musical Arranger — Arrangers work for TV, film, theatre, music publishers and the recording industry, generally in a freelance capacity. Earnings will vary enormously, with the top arrangers earning money from royalties. Arrangers take musical compositions and arrange or adapt them to different styles. They need to be aware of both instrument and voice.

Orchestrator — An orchestrator takes a musical score and transposes it to suit different musical instruments and voices. They sell their services to orchestras, choral groups, theatres and performing artists.

Conductor — A professional conductor conducts large orchestras during both rehearsal and performance. Conductors may be hired for bands, orchestras, chamber music groups, youth orchestras or even school band performances. The top conductors can earn hundreds of thousands of pounds a year. A **Choral Director** conducts and directs singing groups during rehearsal and performances. They may also organise tours.

Music Director — Music directors work for film and TV companies. They are in charge of making sure that the right music is put to a production. They hire composers, musicians and other staff as needed. Some similar skills are used by **Music Teachers** or **Cantors.**

Wedding Singer — A wedding singer sings popular songs for an audience sometimes as part of a band. They may earn an income purely through this or also as a cabaret singer or pub singer/musician. Or some may find work as back-up artists or by doing studio sessions. Perhaps this may even be a starting point for a pop, rock, folk or musical career.

Taste and smell make me feel good

Wallow in your senses in these aromatic careers.

CLASSIC COOL

Baker/Patissiere — Do you long to smell fresh bread early in the morning, or own your own bakery or patisserie? This could easily turn into an uncool career if you are making run-of-the mill breads and cakes. But think more specialist and suddenly you are cool. A few bakers make breads for the connoisseur, such as Italian intergrale, pugliese, stirato, Chinese doughnuts, Persian flatbreads and traditional country cakes. If you can find your niche with a shop or café-cum-shop you can set up an independent and very cool career.

Chocolate Maker — Consumable art is very fashionable, and the film *Chocolat* alerted much of the world to the wonderful career of a professional chocolate maker. A chocolatier creates individual chocolates or chocolate art for restaurants, chocolate shops or cafes.

Tea/Coffee Taster — Tea and coffee companies continually need to research blends of beverages that will satisfy consumers' growing sophisticated tastes. A professional taster samples different blends, using their highly tuned senses in the same way as a professional wine taster or perfumier. They then help to decide which blends to choose for sale.

Perfumier — It is tough to be an independent perfumer in the UK, easier to work for a big perfume house. Perfumiers invent perfumes. You need a good nose and training. **Perfume Historians** are even rarer. They rescue old perfumes and re-create them. Some even search out perfumes from ancient times. It is a very cool career but one that needs financial backing for great marketing in a very competitive industry.

Cake Decorator — Cake decorators use icing and accessories to make and decorate cakes for special events, such as weddings and birthdays. They work for professional cake retailers and in their own businesses. Jane Asher is well known in the cake-decorating field.

Head/Executive Chef — Would you like to be the next Gordon Ramsay or Jamie Oliver? The path to celebrity chef is paved with twelve-hour days, overseeing food deliveries, planning menus and preparing food. Early in your career, it will be fast-paced with poor pay. But, if you can climb as far as an executive chef, the world could be your oyster. You will plan menus, and may create and make recipes, as well as direct the work of kitchen staff, order food supplies and run budgets. An executive chef may run more than one kitchen in a hotel or a big dining operation. If your food is distinctive, you may attract a celebrity clientele and fame and fortune. You'll need a good sense of taste and smell, efficiency and high personal hygiene standards. Training is usually on the job or in vocational institutions.

Private Household Cook — A private household cook prepares meals in private homes. It may be useful to have a cooking speciality or know about specialist dietary or nutritional needs. A similar career is that of **Owner of a Food Business** for a private group of people or corporate body, for example, an employee dining room, hotel, hospital, club or restaurant.

Research Chef — A research chef prepares food with the knowledge of food science, testing new recipes, trying out new flavours, researching the visual appeal of food as well as its nutritional content. They work for food manufacturers and processors, chains of restaurants and food growers.

Sommelier — A wine sommelier selects wine through tastings, and the best may also write about wines. Clearly you need a palate that is finely tuned enough to distinguish blackberry notes from strawberry notes, and a range of vocabulary that is broad enough to articulate the differences among wines from all over the world. You will understand wine quality and food and wine pairings, be able to blind taste and evaluate wines, and know what sells.

Cheesemaker — Goat's, cow's, ewe's, buffalo or vegan soya cheese are all specialities available to the independent cheesemaker. It is, of course, as a food industry, subject to regulation, so be aware of current rules. Otherwise, you need a good palate and a plentiful supply of milk. Train with an existing maker to learn the trade.

VERY COOL

Food/Restaurant Critic — Do you write with flair? Are you a secret foodie? Do you understand what makes good composition in a meal? Could you rate a restaurant against its competitors? A critic will work as a journalist for a newspaper, website or magazine sampling meals in different restaurants, checking facts and filing reviews. A journalistic training, or speciality as a food writer or chef, might be a lead into this career.

I want to create something beautiful

Do you love the visual world? Are you artistic or creative? Can you take an object or place or person and imagine how they could look in the future? Are you skilled with your hands or the computer?

The world of art and design is full of career possibilities, from classic careers such as art, and graphic, interior or fashion design, to more technically skilled design work, such as architecture, computer software design, desktop publishing, landscape design, drafting or engineering.

In the artistic side of this career area, it is more difficult to earn a living. Over 60 per cent of people in artistic careers are self-employed and may never earn their salary purely from this profession. However, enter the computer-aided design world and salaries are higher and employment is more secure. These are some of the coolest careers out there.

CLASSIC COOL

Cartoonist — Most cartoonists are freelance. Formal qualifications matter less for entry to the profession than your portfolio of work. You can find work as the caption-writer or the drawer of the cartoon. Many cartoonists will work for more than one employer and produce single cartoons, cartoon strips or cartoon books.

Costume Designer — A great costume designer is crucial to the success of a film or play. The moment the actor slips on his costume, he finally has the last piece of the jigsaw that lets him create his character. A costume designer creates and overseas the production of original clothes and accessories for films, TV and theatre, and needs to be highly knowledgeable about fabrics and materials.

Set Designer/Decorator — A set designer chooses and designs the sets for theatrical productions, and for TV shows and films. After making themselves familiar both with the script and the director's ideas for the production, they pick a style to suit the tone of the show and make sure the furnishings and set accessories they choose are suitable for the camera crew and actors to work around. A set designer in the theatre will actually build the set, which may include backdrops. They also need to work with the lighting needs of the play.

Wallpaper Designer — A wallpaper designer creates original designs of wallpaper patterns to be sold in shops. As the designer, they may be required to research historic patterns or work to a house style for a particular company. They may also need to select an appropriate production process for the wallpaper and deal with production overseas. **Interior Designers** create a co-ordinated style for a home.

Computer Artist — Computer artists use modern technology to produce artwork for business presentations, advertising, desktop publishing, the media and the publishing industry.

VERY COOL

Fashion Designer — Fashion designers produce original designs and may work in a specialist area, such as menswear or shoes. They study trends and sketch out ideas before choosing the materials and producing the final design. Increasingly many designers use Computer-Aided Design (CAD) in the production process. Designers may make women's, men's or children's wear, or a particular style of wear such as maternity wear, hosiery, scarves or other accessories. About a quarter of designers are self-employed, according to one recent survey. The others work for mass-market retailers, wholesalers, design firms or in the high-fashion industry. **Milliners/Hat Designers** create original designs either working for a shop or as a self-employed designer.

Tattoo Artist/Remover — Tattoos have become so fashionable and widespread that nowadays it is arguably even cooler to be the person who removes tattoos. Tattoo artists draw a basic design on a person using a stencil, and then ink it in using a specialist electric tool. The best create highly original designs. If you want a more temporary art form, how about considering becoming a **Henna Artist**? Many artists are self-employed.

Window Dresser — Also known as a display designer, this career involves planning and designing what goes into the windows and shop fronts of shops and other businesses. Clearly it involves creativity, but also needs an awareness of what will attract business. Certificates in Visual Merchandising are approved by the British Display Society. You can also gain experience through exhibitions.

Animator — Animators and other multimedia artists work in the film and video industry, as well as areas such as computer games or advertising. They make special effects, storyboards for commercials, animated features and one-off characters. They draw by hand, use computers or other materials. Of course, for a really cool career, take your portfolio and head to Hollywood.

Medical Illustrator — Scientific illustrators need both precise drawing skills and a knowledge of a particular area, such as anatomy or biology. A medical illustrator will draw pictures of the human body and medical techniques. Other scientific illustrators may draw anything from planets to molecules or animals. Illustrations are used for publications, audiovisual aids or even for legal evidence. Or, for an appreciative but slightly younger audience, how about becoming a **Children's Book Illustrator**?

Sketch Artist — Sketch artists work with the police to create a portrait of a criminal suspect. They sketch using pencil or charcoal. Sketches are also used in the courtroom where, by law, it is not possible to photograph the accused, the jury or the witnesses in a case. Sketch artists also produce pastel or pencil sketches as portraits for sale to the general public or on commission.

Five top tips for a sense-able creative career

1. **Be rich and creative.** Creativity is often associated with poverty, but this doesn't have to be true.

2. **Creative people are often self-employed.** This gives you scope to get creative about how to earn money as well as about what you produce creatively. An employed career is always limited in terms of what it will earn you. Use a bit of your creativity to be entrepreneurial too.

3. **Challenge yourself.** Creative careers are never boring. They are careers in which you turn hobbies and passions into output, or take the normal and make something new out of it. Damien Hirst is a classic example of a creative who did something challenging to people's perception by using a dead shark as art. How can you challenge your own, or other people's, way of thinking?

4. **Use your creativity for innovation.** Bill Gates is an example of a creative person who has used his creativity to innovate in business. By continually improving and inventing, he has led the competition for years and made a huge amount of money in the process. How could you use your creativity to build a career with a business advantage over your competitors?

5. **Be different.** What's the point of being creative if you follow the crowd? Dare to stand out. Do the opposite of what other people do. Try new things, take a conventional career and give it a twist. See what new creative career you can invent.

* UNUSUALLY COOL

Home Stager –
Home staging started in America. The House Doctor, Ann Maurice, is the UK's most famous home stager. Home stagers prepare houses and other properties for sale and resale by getting rid of clutter and using accessories to make the rooms more pleasing to the eye. Some will even bring in rented furniture if it adds to the potential value of the home. They charge either an hourly rate or a set fee. Home stagers are likely to be self-employed, though some will link up with estate agents, property or interior design companies. Some home stagers now run training courses. Search on the web for contacts.

In the know
Celebrity Starter Careers

Chris Evans started his broadcasting career in radio in Manchester and as a pub DJ. After working as a producer, he went on to work in radio in London as a producer and then a presenter.

Harrison Ford, known best as Indiana Jones, got poor grades at high school and didn't have much success early on as an actor either. Frustrated with his career, he spent some time as a carpenter before winning the role of Han Solo in *Star Wars* in 1977.

Morgan Freeman served as a mechanic in the US Air Force in the 1950s.

Donna Karan, the designer, was introduced to fashion young. Her mother was a model and her father a tailor. Donna worked in a boutique as a teenager and later became an assistant to the designer Anne Klein, becoming the company's chief designer after Klein's death.

Stephen King was an avid reader and sent off his first stories to a publisher when he was only twelve. His first published story was at the age of 19 but, for several years, he had to teach English at a high school to make money.

8. Living off your wits

What are humans without the ability to think? Some of the coolest careers are all in the brain. There are many career ideas out there for the natural thinker. But how do you know if you are one?

Try these for size:

- You are naturally curious, analytical or inquisitive
- You may be good at dealing with theories or data
- Perhaps you enjoy research
- You could be of a scientific turn of mind – observant, precise and logical
- You may love creative thinking or forming complex philosophical theories.

If this is you, these cool careers will all demand that you make full use of your impressive brain power.

I want to look at the big picture

Big-picture thinkers can command some of the most interesting thinking careers. If you would like to forecast future trends, develop a new product, work out a political strategy, or think abstractly, first of all you need to think strategically about your own career.

CLASSIC COOL

Social Psychologist — All aspects of interactions between people are of interest to a social psychologist. How do groups influence behaviour? What makes a consumer buy a product? How can you change a prejudice? You might advise an advertising agency or government, or carry out research in a business or academic environment.

Demographer — Demography is the study of human populations. It looks at population dynamics and subjects such as population distribution and migration or how other relationships between economic, cultural and social factors influence a particular group. Demographers are often employed by the government.

Evolutionary Psychologist — Evolutionary psychology focuses on how the theory of evolution affects human thought and behaviour. Consider, for example, what effect mutation, mating or natural selection have on the way we are today. You will need to be a good researcher, be able to get to grips with the big picture and understand analysis and data.

Political Scientist — Political scientists generally work in the academic world, seeking solutions to political problems and producing theories on topics, such as the structure of government, international relations or social reform. Their expertise is used by politicians, though they do not run for election themselves. They may become TV pundits or print media commentators. Public administration, law or international relations are good backgrounds for this career.

Health Economist — Health economics is playing an increasingly important role in shaping policy on health care in many developed and developing countries. A health economist may work in the public sector or on the pharmaceutical industry to research and develop health management programmes, addressing factors such as the cost-effectiveness of particular treatments and population change using mathematical models.

Business Strategist — The term business strategist may be used quite loosely but, in effect, a business strategist may work inside a business or as an outside advisor to create business, brand, organisational and operational strategies for the overall company or at divisional or departmental levels. They may use a particular model or methodology. An MBA is a useful starting point.

* UNUSUALLY COOL

Retail Strategist –
Shop critics barely existed a few years ago, yet in the 21st century we are all avid consumers. The few retail strategists now out there teach shops how to seduce the shopper into spending money in their stores. They need to understand the competition, the psychology of buying, packaging and advertising. There is no clear route into this profession. Test your sales skills by selling yourself to the business.

Dating Strategist –
This century is spawning a wealth of strategists. A dating strategist provides a service to the single and

lonely. They might teach their clients relationship strategies, explain how to improve their body language, perhaps even matchmake or own a dating agency. This is clearly a self-made, self-employed profession.

Wealth Strategist –

Whereas a few years ago we were all urged to see a financial adviser about establishing sensible personal financial habits, nowadays there are advisers who want to teach us how to build large amounts of wealth, rather than simply follow a conservative saving or investment strategy. If you want to call yourself a wealth strategist, you'll need to find personal replicable strategies that allow you to mentor others in creating wealth. You can specialise in an area, such as property, or build your own unique niche.

Global Currency Strategist –

Some of the bigger global banks employ strategists to take account of policy affecting their business and profits. A currency strategist helps the bank and its clients to forecast trends and to make moves into different foreign exchanges, according to economic trends and geopolitical developments. This is a fast-paced, long-hours job that involves research and solid investment expertise.

Property Strategist –

A professional property expert understands the psychology of property. More than an estate agent, they can do everything from tell you how to make your house more sellable, to deal with estate agents, or find you a property for a fee. **Property Finders** will give you part *of this service but there is a demand for a fuller service from many professionals.*

I am fascinated by words and language

Many ideas-people also love working in the world of language. They enjoy writing or even thinking about the structure or sound of words and language. If you want a cool career in this area, start your thinking right here.

CLEARLY COOL

Technical Writer — A technical writer writes manuals, handbooks and guides on how to operate computer software and programs. The key is to distil something that appears very complicated into text that is easy to read. If you have ever struggled to make head or tail of a manual for your new gadget, you will know just how much need there is out there! The good thing about this career is that there are opportunities all over the world, in small companies and in large. Your work doesn't even need to be published; you could just write for your office.

Cognitive Psychologist — A cognitive psychologist is interested in cognition, memory, reasoning, perception and judgement. They often work with neuroscientists. Cognitive psychologists try to understand information processing, for example – how people understand and answer problems. In recent years they have looked at parallels between the human brain and artificial computer intelligence.

Greeting Card Writer — All those rhymes and witty (or not so witty) jokes in cards are written by professional writers for card manufacturers. It is a very niche and probably self-employed profession, but an interesting and creative one for a poet or professional writer. Build up a personal portfolio and contact card companies directly with examples of your work.

News Journalist — A journalist either writes for newspapers or broadcasts on the radio or television. You need to have a particular interest, either in news or in a particular area, such as health or science. The best way into this career is through specific college or university training as a journalist. You need to have good writing skills, of course, but you also need to be able to write copy quickly and accurately.

Magazine Writer — A magazine writer is able to write in a particular style that suits the target readership of a magazine. As a magazine journalist, you need great research and journalism skills and the ability to come up with fresh ideas for articles. If you aren't trained as a journalist, find your entry point as a specialist in a particular subject, such as fashion or travel.

Web-content Developer — A web content writer/ developer writes and edits information online. They work like a journalist, creating text as well as working with photographs and graphics. They may work freelance for a number of clients or be employed by a big company to produce external and internal communications.

Copy and Ad Writer — If you are great at thinking up new ideas, a good writer and creative with it, then this could be a wonderful career for you. Your copy will be used to describe products to sell them on the web, TV, newspapers, magazines or even for the radio.

VERY COOL

Storyteller — Professional storytellers tell stories to an audience. They believe that the oral tradition and narrative can enhance the lives of an audience. There has been a rebirth of the art over the last three decades. Professional storytellers perform in libraries, in schools and on the stage. Now storytelling has also been taken into the workplace as a tool for making sure good practice is communicated throughout a company.

Drama Coach — A drama coach teaches and coaches actors to interpret scripts and characters, and helps on specific issues, such as voice, dialect and how to have stage charisma. The **Dialogue**, **Accent** and **Vocal Coach** also work in similar areas.

Master of ceremonies — An MC is a professional events entertainer. They may provide services for entertainment events, corporate events or weddings. Their primary duty is to be a cool, level-headed and genial host or hostess. They provide the link between performers and clients, keep the event on time and make announcements. If this appeals to you, look for advertisements for MCs and toastmasters.

Speechwriter — A speechwriter writes speeches for politicians, business leaders, weddings or events. This can be a stand-alone career, or you may also work in public relations or be a professional scriptwriter for film or TV. Some speechwriters come to the area through joke-telling. A good stand-up comedian may contribute to a speechwriting team for celebrity clients including MPs.

Ventriloquist — A ventriloquist creates illusion for the ear. They fool an audience into perceiving, if not believing, that an object or puppet is talking, rather than the ventriloquist. They entertain audiences and normally have a comic routine as a key part of the act. If you want to become a ventriloquist, you will need to train yourself and get out there on the comedy or variety circuit.

✳ *UNUSUALLY COOL*

Archivist of Unusual Languages and Unusual Dialects -

There are many different languages and dialects in the world. But, just as animals are endangered by the relentless onslaught of modern society, so are some of the lesser-spoken languages. Archivists research these and make sure that they record examples to be used by academics and researchers.

Graphologist -

A graphologist analyses handwriting in order to produce a personality profile of the writer. They are sometimes used in business for recruitment or as a way of identifying a criminal suspect. Graphologists believe that you can read someone's mental state from their handwriting.

Cryptoanalyst -

A cryptoanalyst breaks codes for the security services, the police or other agencies. They use computers and other tools to find out how messages have been encoded to hide their secrets. Mathematics is an ideal background for this career.

In the know
Celebrity Starter Careers

Jamie Oliver started his career at the famous River Café in west London.

Judy Finnegan was born in 1948 and began her career at Granada Television as a researcher in 1971 before moving to Anglia TV in Norwich as a reporter. Her husband **Richard Madeley** began his career in an Essex local newspaper before becoming a news producer and presenter at BBC Radio Carlisle. He subsequently moved to Border Television as a reporter and then to Yorkshire and Granada TV.

Helen Mirren, the Oscar-winning actress, is the granddaughter of a Russian aristocrat. She has said that one of her previous jobs was working in Southend-on-Sea at an amusement park, where she had to persuade people to use the rides.

Early in his career, **Brad Pitt** hid his good looks under a chicken costume to invite customers to visit a fast-food restaurant.

9. Down and dirty

Most people might say they want to reach for the stars, but maybe you're the sort of person who would rather roll around in the mud? Are you the type of person who would rather be doing things than talking about things? Do you like getting physical? Perhaps you prefer handling things to delving into data. Or maybe you would rather use your body rather than your brain to forge a career. If so, consider a practical, hands-on or physical career.

I like to get my hands dirty

How hands-on are you? Could your hands be your tools? Would you like to make something from a physical material? If so, consider working in areas such as mechanics or engineering, repairing things, farming, carpentry or any hands-on design job. Here are a few cool alternatives.

PRACTICAL, HANDS-ON COOL

Floral Designer — Most floral designers learn on the job and can expect to work long hours, and at weekends and holidays. They make displays out of live and dried flowers for weddings, gifts and decorations. Most work in small independent shops, though some work for wholesale flower distributors or internet florists. **Landscape Architects** also work with flowers and plants, as do **Greenhouse and Nursery Workers.**

Garden Designer — Garden designers draw up and plant out designs for small or big gardens owned by private individuals, companies or the heritage sector. Some garden designers come from a botany background. Others may specialise in restoring or developing historic gardens so may have a particular interest in researching a historic designer, or plants from a particular region or period.

Blacksmith — A blacksmith forges iron and steel and shapes it into items such as wrought-iron objects, furniture, tools and weapons. They heat the metal and use tools to beat, bend and cut it. A blacksmith who makes and fits horseshoes is known as a **Farrier.**

Sculptor — It is difficult to earn a living as a sculptor, so you many end up teaching or working part-time. There is no standard career path, though a fine art degree may set you on the right track. Some sculptors specialise in big commissioned public space works; others sell work through galleries and shops. Wood, bronze, marble and steel are all popular materials.

Stone Carver — A stone carver follows a design and carves it on to a stone such as granite. Some stone carvers may make their own designs. They are commissioned to make memorials and gravestones. Some are employed by the memorial industry directly.

Silversmith/Goldsmith — A silver or goldsmith uses specialist equipment to create large and small items from sheet metal. Some work in jewellery shops. Others are commissioned to produce one-off pieces. Training usually comes on the job by working with a mentor. Salaries vary widely and most silver/goldsmiths are self-employed or work part-time.

Book/Paper Restorer — Museums, libraries and collectors employ specialist restorers in the print and paper trade to maintain historical and artistic documents. Restorers treat, preserve and restore the paper using techniques such as dry and wet cleaning and retouching.

Toymaker — Traditional toymakers make toys by hand. Some toymakers specialise in restoring antique toys. Others work as toy designers for large companies creating modern toys for manufacturing companies and high-street shops. You need an understanding of materials and practical work, and legal safety standards and good business skills to promote your work if you are self-employed.

Glass-blower — Glass-blowers blow glass to create art for medical or scientific purposes. Artists are often self-employed, but scientific glass-blowers are employed by research laboratories where they have to work with great precision producing glass to particular specifications for dimensions and durability. Glass engraving is a linked art.

Topiarist — Any kind of gardening means getting your hands dirty. Topiarists are professional gardeners or landscape architects who work with trees, hedges and bushes to make living sculptures. Lesser known is the **Facial Topiarist**, who trims beards and moustaches in exotic ways. However, he is unlikely to make much of a career of it!

Lighting Director — Lighting directors design and set the lights for performances in the theatre, events, film and TV. They need to make the actors and presenters look attractive and natural, light up the action and produce special effects. They may be electricians. The money can be very good. In the US, where the major studios are based, a lighting director can make up to $110,000 with overtime. Rock bands and popstars also need lighting directors for tours.

* *UNUSUALLY COOL*

Yurt/Igloo Maker –
Housing is where we can all personally get a little greener. Yurts are the sustainable form of housing used in Mongolia, which can be erected easily, rather like a gigantic tent. Igloos are, of course, used by Eskimos. There are a few craftsmen in the world who use steam bending as an environmentally friendly way of re-forming wood to make versions of these as green homes.

I like things as much as (or more than) people

Many practical people prefer getting results in their careers focusing on things rather than people. If you think things are fun, consider a career as an engineer, a carpenter, working with equipment, cars or planes, or how about being an electrician, a technician, surveyor, or working in the telecommunications or computer industries? Also take a look at the adrenalin charged careers in Chapter 4 – most of these need practical skills.

CLASSIC COOL

Retouch Specialist — A retouching specialist colour corrects, silhouettes and retouches photos. These are the people who make celebrities look perfect for the magazines. Art, photography or graphic design is a good background to get you started in this career.

Ergonomicist — Ergonomics is the industry that studies the interaction of humans and machines, for example, how to use equipment such as computer keyboards, desks and chairs to prevent strain on the muscles, tendons and joints of workers. The need for this type of role keeps on growing, but many people are not yet aware of this area. **Health and Safety Advisor** is a linked career.

Engineering Psychologist — If you are interested in people and things, this could be your perfect career. How can a person work at a computer most efficiently? What is the best way to make sure you don't burn out at work? Engineering psychologists are employed by industry and the government to optimize the relationship between people and the things they work with, and advise on how to prevent problems from occurring.

Engraver — This is very detailed, patient work, which requires an individual style. Engravers are commissioned or use their own designs to engrave images on to wood, glass or metal. Some engraving is done by machinery now, but you can work on a self-employed basis selling individual craftworks to galleries or occasionally to a large company.

Printmaker — Printmakers use a printing press to print an image in ink on paper or material. They also use computers and hand printing. Printmakers use their own or other people's designs. Designs may be cut or etched using different materials including metal or wood.

Museum Curator — Nowhere are you going to be surrounded by more beautiful things than in one of the top museums of the world. For a similar career at a possibly more local level, look at managing or running an art or craft gallery.

VERY COOL

Stunt Flyer — Stunt flyers are professional pilots who perform stunts for public entertainment or the TV or movie industry. **Commercial Pilots** may not sound quite as cool, but being a pilot of any kind is still one of the most aspirational careers out there.

Microbrewer — Microbrewery owners produce traditional cask ale. These small breweries operate on the basis of making quality ales to compete with the large mass-market breweries. The industry has grown in the USA, Canada, Australia and New Zealand since the 1970s and looks set to remain popular.

Stained-glass Artist — Glass artists draw their own designs and cut and stain glass to make works of art on commission or for sale to shops and galleries. They are in demand from churches and collectors. This career may demand research and sensitivity to the architecture in which the glass is being used and a knowledge of history and religion.

Musical Instrument Maker — Specialising in a particular area, you may take on commissions for making a woodwind or brass instrument or a more unusual instrument, or take on repairs. You need strong technical skills and a background in woodwork, metalwork or technical drawing. It's an insecure profession, though. Most makers and repairers are self-employed.

* *UNUSUALLY COOL*

Racing Car Driver –

Becoming a racing car driver is only an option for the coolest. Formula Ford, Formula 3 British Touring Cars, Le Mans 24-Hours, Champ Car World Series, Formula Renault, British GT – you'll need a racing licence and a medical to enter any race. In the UK, the Motor Sports Association (MSA) governs all car circuit racing. The best way to start is to go to racetracks and talk directly to the competitors at local circuits about how they got started. Volunteer for any role at a local track that is available. Finally, grab 'seat time' in a kart/car or any vehicle that's available.

I want to make money from my body

Can you use your body to make money? Well, yes. Why not, after all, you were born with it. Relax, though, we are talking moral, legal and pain free. The obvious way to make money from your body is from sport. For sport lovers, fitness fanatics and lovers of the body beautiful, there are more and more ways to make money and keep fit at the same time. You can sell your ability to do a sport directly or indirectly; teach a sport or form of fitness; or work in a related field like agenting.

Another way to sell your body is to be a model, but there are ways to make money from your body even if you are not blessed with the looks of a Naomi Campbell or Kate Moss. Some cool body careers are occasional opportunities for the portfolio worker; others have the makings of a more consistent career.

GET PHYSICAL

Surf Instructor — For those who thought it was just a Californian thing, yes, there really are surf schools in the UK. The British Surfing Association is the governing body that rates different schools and trains surf coaches. So, if you would like to make money from your rippled muscles, this could be your career.

Glamour Model — Glamour models are usually nude or semi-nude models in erotic poses. It generally manages to avoid being considered mainstream porn, as sex acts are not shown. Models may be topless or wear skimpy clothing, but do not show their genitalia. Would-be models should contact agencies but must be clear on what they will and will not show!

Mime Artist — Marcel Marceau is one of the most famous mime artists of the last fifty years; Rowan Atkinson is an actor with considerable miming skills. Mime artists use their body gestures, facial expressions and acting without using their voice to portray characters and storylines. Consider approaching a talent agent to find event and theatrical work.

Life Model — A life model must be able to hold poses over a period of up to three hours with breaks and changes of position. Looks are less important, as is gender. They are in demand at art colleges, schools or for professional sculptors and artists. Models can make up to £10 per hour.

Film/TV Extra — Any look can be in demand for extra work. It requires no great talent, though may involve lots of sitting or standing around. However, many extras love getting close to the stars. Sign up with an agency, but look around – some charge up-front fees.

Hand/Foot/Leg/Hair Model — Even if you aren't beautiful, maybe a bit of you is? If you have beautiful hands, legs or hair, or a perfect six-pack, you can make money. A top advert model can make hundreds of pounds per week.

Hair Selling — With the trend for hair extensions among celebrities and the ongoing need for hair for wigs and hairpieces for beauty and medical reasons, good quality hair is always in demand. Much commercial hair comes from Asia or Eastern Europe. However, you could sell your hair for several pounds an ounce. It needs to be at least six inches long and untreated chemically.

In the know
Celebrity Starter Careers

J. K. Rowling, the author of Harry Potter, was a teacher and a researcher for a charity before her children's stories were published.

William Shatner was a trained dancer at the National School of Canada before becoming Captain Kirk.

Steven Spielberg produced his first film at the age of twelve and won a prize for his short war film *Escape to Nowhere* at thirteen. At 16, he showed his first feature-length sci-fi film *Firelight* in a local cinema. At college he won festival success with a short film, winning him a job as a television director with Universal – the opportunity that indirectly led him to his later success on *Jaws*, a film that grossed $260 million.

Sting was a teacher before becoming a singer.

Martha Stewart once planned birthday parties for a living.

10. Striking it rich

Money, money, money. Some people just to want to be rich, and that's OK. Some of the highest achievers on the planet are motivated by wealth rather than altruism.

Is it enough to have a steady income that grows over time, or do you want more? Maybe you just want to be a little bit better off than your friends and family, pay all your bills and save for a rainy day. Do you yearn for a life of luxury? Do you have debts to pay off in a hurry? How long are you prepared to wait for the rewards from all your hard work? Or perhaps you want to buy a house mortgage free, drink champagne every day and take holidays in the world's top resorts.

These are the careers that will make you rich.

Cool courses that will make you rich

Getting rich is a habit that begins young. Start by thinking early on about what you study. According to a recent study, the earning power of your degree varies by more than £300,000 depending on what you study at university. These are some of the courses that will earn you the most in your career:

1. Medicine

2. Engineering

3. Maths and computer science

4. Environmental and physical science

5. Architecture

6. Business

7. Social science and law

    And just so you know, some of the courses that
    will earn you less than average in your career are:

1. Biosciences

2. European languages

3. Humanities

4. Arts

I don't care what I do, just show me the money

'I need to pay off my debts'
'I just want to earn more than my friends'
'I don't care what I do as long as it is well paid'

If this is you, what careers are out there that hit the cool bar purely through the potential for generating a fat wad of cash?

COOL CASH

Sports Coach — A top sports coach can travel all over the world and make a six or even seven-figure salary. His more ordinary cousin, the **Personal Trainer**, can still make good money though at a significantly reduced level. The average personal trainer at a gym makes about £30,000 but, if you get into management and set up a personal training business with several trainers, expect to see your earnings rise rapidly.

Commercial Real Estate — Outside the world of selling houses, the job of leasing and managing commercial properties can pull in big bucks. Real-estate developers need heads of construction, sales managers and general managers.

Council Chief Executive — In the financial year 2005–2006, two hundred local council employees earned more than £100,000. The top-earning chief executive was in London and earned nearly £230,000. As a comparison, the Prime Minister earned £186,429.

Advertising Professional — Advertising professionals, such as account managers, product managers and creative directors, can expect to have a good lifestyle with their earnings.

Technical Writer — If you can develop a specialisation, for example, in professional writing for the financial or software industry, technical writing jobs can be well paid. A good technical writer can take a complex subject, such as pension or high-tech issues, and make it understandable to a lay reader. Many of these positions are freelance.

* UNUSUALLY COOL

Professional Coach –
Business and life coaches (life trainers rather than body trainers) can be even better paid. It seems that we are willing to pay more to have our relationships and career sorted out than we are to have our bodies toned. The top salaries are still in the States where the fashion started – about 20 per cent of coaches there earn six figure incomes, according to estimates from industry watchers. Although various professional associations are being started, no special degree or training is required. The key to six-figure success in coaching is finding a speciality and sticking with it.

American Casino Manager –
A casino general manager isn't quite all it looks like in all those films about Las Vegas, but your responsibility is rewarded with a good salary. The general manager (GM) of a casino takes care of the gambling business of an operation and also any restaurants and hotel associated with it. It's a people business so you'll need to be a good manager, be able to get results at the bottom line and, also, to understand customer service. Most casinos don't work nine to five, so expect sixty-hour weeks spreading over weekends and holiday periods.

QUESTIONABLY COOL

Lap Dancer — If you want to earn money in a hurry, lap dancing is seen as a popular way to get cash. It isn't always the dead cert it seems, though. Lap dancers usually pay the club a fee for each shift that they work, so could make a loss. However, top girls in top city venues can make hundreds of pounds a night. High-class escorts can earn £1,000 a night or more.

I deserve a six (or seven) figure salary

One way to really safeguard your future is to aim to earn over £100,000 a year. Even with tax, you'll be able to save money, tackle the property market with a smile on your face, and hold your head up high amongst your peers.

If you reach that £100,000 a year mark, you'll be among the privileged few. Less than half a per cent of people in the UK earn a six-figure salary. In fact, in 2006, the median weekly pay for full-time employees was under £500 a week, and the median for female employees was even less. Earnings in London are higher, and lower in the northeast of England. But, just because these salaries are unusual, it doesn't mean that they are impossible to obtain. You don't always need a mass of qualifications to earn a lot either. Often experience and drive will get you to the six-figure mark as quickly as a degree.

In truth, many of those who reach six figures go on to earn much, much more. Some earn millions out of a combination of salary, bonus and stocks, often with other perks thrown in as well. So, how can you beat the odds and make sure you get to be the person who earns six figures or more?

VERY COOL

Private Dentist — All those British bad teeth have to be rectified somewhere and the money for those new veneers goes straight into a six-figure salary.

Surgeon — You'll need steady hands and high level medical skills to be a surgeon, but all those years of training will pay off in personal income terms.

Petroleum Engineer — Where there is energy there has always been wealth. From the oil barons of yesteryear to engineers today, a high income is there for the taking.

Lawyer — We all know the high hourly rates a lawyer can charge. It is no urban myth: lawyers do indeed make pots of money.

Company Director — The top earners in the UK are company directors. In fact, for a good number theirs aren't just six-figure but seven-figure salaries. The CEO of a top company like Marks & Spencer or Tesco will have a total salary package of well over a million. Even in the public sector, the CEO of a company like Network Rail walks off with over half a million.

Doctor — Doctors are one of the best-paid professions in the UK. The average GP's salary is now over £80,000 and many hit the six-figure mark.

Head Teacher — If you look at the bare figures this looks like a good choice. But beware, though a few head teachers can earn over £100,000, some earn only £40,000.

Footballer — If you become a top footballer, you can expect more, more, more. Not only will you rake in an impressively huge salary, but also bonuses and, of course, lucrative sponsorship deals. David Beckham has reputedly made over £13 million from his salary and business deals. Your career may be as short as those in that other notoriously rich yet fickle profession, pop singing, but invest well and you will not only make money quickly but also continue to lead a champagne lifestyle for a long time. Don't forget the **Football Manager**. A top-of-his-game football manager like Alex Ferguson can expect to take home millions each year. Or look at being a **Football Agent.**

Sports Professional — Other sports have similarly big earning potential, though this could require international travel. If you are tall and skilled with a ball, head over to the States and make millions as a basketball player, or why not see if you can make it in baseball. In the UK, golf is worth big money at the top levels of the game. Top players like golfer Colin Montgomerie can make over a million from tournaments and sponsorship. Taking up tennis can pay off too. A top umpire will only earn about £60,000 but a Tim Henman-level player can also hit the seven-figure mark.

CITY COOL

If you want to make really big money, though, go to where money is the product. The money-making centres of the world, including the City of London, are a first stop if you want to beat the odds on pay.

The average male median pay in the City is now just over £100,000. In some companies that is also the average across all company staff. When you think that this figure includes everyone from the man who washes the floors to the CEO, it shows just how high some City salaries are. Working in one of the financial centres of the world will give you a good chance of making a six-figure salary. If you want to make seven figures, the careers below will ensure you get really, really well paid. We're talking big salaries and mega bonuses.

Institutional Fund Manager — A fund manager invests money in a portfolio of stocks and other investments. He or she may specialise in the type of investment or in a region in which he/she invests. They are in charge of tens or hundreds of millions of pounds of pension fund, unit and investment trust money. They are directly rewarded for their performance.

Personal Financial Adviser — Becoming a personal financial adviser or financial planner isn't as sure a route to a six-figure salary as some City jobs. It depends on the wealth of your client base, as well as your advisory skills. Financial advisers advise individuals on subjects, such as investments, retirement planning, estate planning and tax management. They may also buy and sell products such as ISAs, stocks or insurance. You can specialise in one financial product or a broad range. The key is to make commission and to build a solid reputation. This is certainly a career that can see you through to retirement.

Interdealer Broker — An interdealer broker acts as an intermediary between market makers (traders in bonds and derivatives). This is a hectic job where you have to constantly keep an eye on market activity and pricing and be quick to react to moves. The better your deals, the more money you will make personally. But, if you want this career, realise it is high reward, high burn-out. Don't expect to be doing it when you are sixty. Start young, retire young.

Hedge Fund Manager — It has become every City worker's dream to make a few million while gambling hundreds of millions of other people's money. Now there are reputedly more than 8,000 hedge funds in a $1 trillion industry, many of which are still remarkably unknown. A hedge fund is a very flexible fund that can use a wide variety of financial instruments to reduce its risk of investment in the stock market. Most hedge funds are managed by highly specialised and experienced investment professionals and invested in by private banks, high net worth individuals, pension funds and insurance companies. The money rewards can be huge. In the USA, hedge fund managers have made up to £1.5 billion profit in a year; in the UK, over £50 million. That is far more than the top directors of even the world's largest financial companies like Goldman Sachs, and certainly much, much more than the CEO of a Marks & Spencer or Diageo.

Stockbroker — Stockbrokers recommend investments to buy and sell in equities, bonds, money and different financial products for their clients. They may provide investment services for private clients or for institutional investors. They work within investment management companies and specialist stockbroking companies and have direct contact with clients. The Association of Private Client Investment Managers and Stockbrokers (APCIMS) has members among both private client and institutional stockbrokers.

Private Equity Investor — The world of private equity has hit the headlines as investors have bought stakes in well-known companies. Investors invest medium and long-term finance either for venture capital or buyouts. This has become a very rich industry, yet surprisingly, many of the big companies are not household names, primarily because investor privacy has been paramount. One of the most successful in Europe is currently Permira.

Five warnings for City slickers

The money in the City is great, but the lifestyle comes with a big health warning:

1. **Many City careers have long hours.** 70–80 hours a week (or more) is often the norm .

2. **There will be lots of travel, which isn't good for work–life balance or healthy romantic relationships.** You'll need to visit clients and companies, which means global travel in this 24-hour business world.

3. **There's always pressure to meet deadlines.** The markets are fast-moving and no one waits for you to catch up.

4. **You often need to be good at sales and marketing.** Doing business with clients is part and parcel of many of these careers. As well as being good at what you do, you need to learn to talk a good game as well.

5. **Personal qualities are as important as academic qualifications.** If you don't have a strong will to succeed, self-confidence and the ability to handle rejection (frequently), these are unlikely to be the careers for you.

What I really want is the champagne lifestyle

It may be that raw cash is not as important to you as the lifestyle it will buy. Do you love to eat at expensive restaurants, stay at top-tier hotels and live life luxuriously? Earning a top salary or doing a senior management job won't guarantee a work life of glamour or excess – you might just get stuck in an office. However, there are a few jobs out there where the good life is part of the package.

CHAMPAGNE COOL

Incentive Company Executive — Incentive travel companies need to check out luxury breaks, hotels and spas that are used to reward high-achieving employees of travel companies or award winners. As an account manager, you will need to travel frequently, try out the incentives and be willing to jump on a plane at short notice. You will need to be on duty, but you will also get to drink cocktails. A travel and tourism qualification can help get you on the first rung of the ladder.

Product/Contract Managers — These are similar roles, in which you will also get to visit hotels and destinations and design holidays.

Commercial Managers — Commercial managers put together profitable travel packages. The highest salaries are in commercial travel agencies. Senior staff can earn up to £60,000. If you want to earn even more (up to £80,000 a year), you could sell global distribution systems software to the travel industry.

Resort/Spa Reviewer — One of the most sought-after pieces of journalism is the beauty and leisure spa review. You get to be pampered for free at the world's top resorts and fawned over by spa staff desperate for a good rating. It's going to be competitive so if you want this cushy little number you'll have to fight it out and win with your journalistic talent, great beauty or travel contacts.

Fashion Journalist — If you are a top fashion journalist, then you will get to hang around the rich and, even if you can't afford their lifestyle, you will expect to get some freebies from designers and industry PRs who want to get their clients in the news. Fashion journalists check out trends, attend press openings and trade shows, interview designers and write features. It's not life right at the top, but it's still pretty cool.

I want the celebrity life by proxy

Following the rich and famous by becoming a celebrity employee is one route to brush against the celebrity lifestyle when you can't afford it yourself. All sorts of people need assistants: politicians, presidents, film directors, authors, film and theatre stars, millionaires, motivational speakers, footballers, footballers' wives and models.

You will have to work hard but you will live in opulent surroundings, often in otherwise inaccessibly expensive parts of the world. You may have unexpected perks, such as cars and gifts, and you are likely to come into contact with some of the richest and most influential people on the world.

Six top tips for celebrity employment

What makes a good assistant to the rich and famous?

1. **Be presentable.** But don't be so glamorous that you outdo the boss.

2. **Stay calm.** You need to be cool in an emergency and good at taking a bit of abuse. How are your skills in finding out obscure bits of information? Is your etiquette up to scratch? Can you manage a household and deal with staff? Could you find the boss's favourite food and drink at 3 a.m.? Are you comfortable getting on the phone to a top politician, or making sure that the hotel chef is au fait with your boss's special dietary requirements?

3. **Keep mum.** Discretion is the byword for every job in every country. Would you be willing to lie to your boss's mother/boyfriend/girlfriend/manager about where your boss is or who she/he is with?

4. **Put your needs last.** Be willing to give your life to your boss. One thing you won't avoid is getting caught up in the drama of your boss's life. Their needs are always first. Yours are last.

And finally:

5. **Don't sell your story to the tabloid press.**

6. **Don't sleep with your boss (or their partner).** Ever! Ever! Ever!

ENTOURAGE COOL

Celebrity Personal Assistant — The job of a celebrity PA on paper meets the high life, high glamour test. After all, you get to meet the rich and famous on an intimate level, you may travel the world and you could earn up to £80,000 a year. Add to this perks like freebies, clothes, first-class travel and some fantastic contacts, and you can see why this could be considered a very cool career. But (and it is a big but) you could well be on call every hour of the day and night, you'll be sworn to confidentiality about every juicy detail of the lives of your clients and, ultimately, be the general dogsbody who has to take care of any detail of your boss's private life. You will meet great contacts but there is no straight line, say, from a job as a CPA to a film star, into the film industry itself. However, if you are good at using that bulging contact book, who knows? Your administrative skills could well be transferable into the film industry as a producer, for example. Check out the website for the USA based Association of Celebrity personal assistants (ACPA) at www.celebrityassistants.org or its UK equivalent UKACA at www.ukaca.org.

Butler — There is a worldwide shortage of top butlers and the classic English gentleman is most in demand. Butlering has made a comeback over recent years, but not in the Jeeves style of yesteryear. Nowadays a butler is likely to work for a hedge fund manager or an entrepreneur. In some ways it is no different from any middle or senior management position, requiring a cool head, and good task and project management skills. As well as waiting at tables and valeting, you will need to be multilingual and IT literate, doing everything from looking after a private office or shopping, to travelling with the family or clients on a private plane. In London a butler can earn £40,000 plus accommodation. Elsewhere in the world, salaries vary from country to country but, at the top end, a head butler in charge of multiple residences for a billionaire could earn up to £250,000. One, it is rumoured, earns over a million.

Super Yacht Skipper — Would you like to see the world from a luxury craft? A life on the high seas could be yours by crewing a yacht for a billionaire. There are more super yachts than ever before, all of which require staff, from stewards to cleaners. But the top position is the captain or skipper. Some yacht positions are seasonal. Some crews are allowed to be informal. Others are uniformed and very formal. Some yachts are used by the owner all year round; others are rented out to clients. To become a yacht skipper it may be useful to gain experience in another area such as the Navy.

Working for Royalty

Working for royalty doesn't just mean standing on a military parade ground or following the Queen with her handbag. Every royal residence needs a wealth of staff to keep it going. Not all the jobs are well paid, but many of the jobs are unique to royalty. And there are some perks associated with the jobs that you won't find elsewhere, often including accommodation. Be aware that you'll need to be security vetted – just to check you are not an undercover reporter.

Jobs are advertised in the press or in *Monarchy Today*. Examples of some Royal roles are:

1. **Art Curator**

2. **Public relations**
    Whether it's the Queen or Prince Charles, modern life requires modern spin.

3. **Maid** or **Housekeeper**

4. **Footman**
    Definitely not a well-paid job, but where else do you get to wear livery nowadays?

5. **Chef**
    You could be preparing meals not only for royalty but for guests, foreign presidents and the rich and famous.

6. **Horticulture**
    All those gardens need lots of attention before and after the garden parties.

7. **Secretary**

8. **Human Resources Manager**

11. Up front and out there

'I want to be the best.'
'I long to be admired.'

Clearly, if you reach the top of anything you are going to appear much cooler than those you have passed by (or pushed down) on the way up. If you want to get to the top, you'll need to be assertive and self-confident, and have popularity and charisma, as well as focus, tenacity, vision and application. However, if you have those skills in bucketloads, you might as well aim for the top of a profession that's worth having.

I want to schmooze for a living

Are you persuasive, energetic, decisive and ambitious? Do you know exactly what you want? Are you determined to get it no matter what other people think?

CLASSIC COOL

Events Planner — This has potential to be cool if you can get into organising interesting events. But events planning can mean anything from a business conference to a party, sports or PR event, university exchange trip, concert or wedding reception. For a cool career it has to be a cool event. The Olympics, anyone?

Public Relations Executive — There are lots of PR jobs out there, so choose wisely. You need exceptional people skills, charm and clear thinking for all those social events. It takes energy to create or maintain a company's image in the media. You could end up copywriting, advising clients, project planning, writing a press release or creating a website, organising a client launch or a lunch. For the coolest careers, start your own agency or represent a cool area such as the environment.

Bank Public Policy Lobbyist — This is a PR job in the wealthiest industry in the UK. Drafting and communicating public policy for a big bank, you'll get to deal with politicians and bank strategists. A little-known job, you might prepare a briefing for the Opposition leader about new financial regulations, or talk to a million-pound trader in your bank about what you need to do to keep the business going.

Politician — Sometimes called showbiz for ugly people, politics nevertheless has the pull of power. While some may dispute a politician's charm, energy is always in demand – from attending constituency parties, campaigning door to door or fighting your corner at Question Time. For national politics you'll need to prove your party loyalty going back years and probably stand as a candidate for an unwinnable constituency before you make it as an MP. Standing as a council member is a good place to find out whether you have the stamina.

Campaigner — Do you have a cause you feel strongly about? Why not become its advocate? Other possibilities include **Freelance Fundraiser.** Check out the Institute of Fundraising. As an independent fundraiser you can work on commission or for a daily flat rate. Your job is to network with individuals or institutions with money and persuade them to donate to the charity you are representing. You may well be an advocate for more than one charity at a time.

VERY COOL

Rickshaw Entrepreneur — Rickshaws used to be associated with early 1920s China. Now they are likely to be found, with a bicycle attached, in major British cities. It requires lots of energy to keep selling your wares on a daily basis. So invest in several vehicles and make money while others pedal.

Spin Doctor — A sub-category of public relations, the term spin doctor is very 21st century and usually refers to political PR. Be prepared for tough scraps with the media. You may be advised to have a career in a PR firm first, while keeping in with a political party. Look to gain some great networking contacts and you might get a foot in the door. If you want a similarly high-profile career, you could consider becoming a **Publicist**, but look along the celebrity Max Clifford route.

Entertainment Reporter — Tracking down the stars and getting the interview before any of your competitor magazines takes grit and tenacity. Running down the runway with a mike attached while working for TV or radio, you also need instant switch-on-able charm so all those celebrities will love you. What's more, everybody wants this career, so start any way you can as a journalist and ask, ask, ask for every opportunity going.

* UNUSUALLY COOL

Ambassador –
This is a career that is hard to achieve, and is only for the intelligent and very aspirational. An ambassador is in charge of diplomatic relations with a particular country and is based overseas for a period of several years. You will have to work your way through the Foreign Office, with no certainty of achieving your goal, but the good news is that there are lots of very cool careers en route. Contact the Foreign Office for details of entry-level career possibilities.

Nudist Spa Owner –
Clearly, running a nudist spa is particularly cool, but being a **Spa Owner** *is also classic cool. Any career in which you have rich guests is going to demand charm and diplomacy. A spa is generally a glamorous destination wherever you are in the world. If you want to up the glam factor a bit then look at onsens in Japan, hot spas in Hungary or exotic resorts in Asia. You will need good tourist and management skills to get into this career.*

I love to show off

Show-offs long to win people over with their talent, gregarious personality or simple charisma. What's more they have some of the coolest careers going.

The upside of a show-off career is that you'll get lots of attention in these careers. Many of these careers are highly creative and most are outside an office environment. That's good for anyone who likes a lot of freedom.

The downside is that you won't always get privacy or necessarily lots of money. And some of these careers demand serious talent from an early age. But, even if you only have a smidgeon of skill, there's a show-off career for you in the lists below.

VISIBLE COOL

Children's Party Entertainer — This job calls for buckets of enthusiasm and a desire to perform. It's casual work and you are likely to be self-employed. If you need money it might be a good idea to have another job as well. But much of the appeal is in the flexible hours and the lack of a boss.

Laser Artist — A laserist or specialist in laser displays creates shows that are generally accompanied by different types of music. Optical shows are put on by big amusement parks or entertainment centres, or self-employed laser artists work freelance putting on one-off displays.

Holiday Resort Representative — Ideal if you need little sleep, are always up for meeting new people in more than one country, and if you are good at finding quick solutions to problems without losing your sense of humour. If you need to pack your job away at night, this is not for you. But, if you want to travel, and possibly have another language, can organise a party and want every day to be unique, this could appeal. Look at tour operators for openings.

Entertainment Park Singer/Dancer/Entertainer — If you have a particular acrobatic, dancing, singing, acting or comedic talent, consider becoming an entertainer at one of the world's big amusement or entertainment parks. The more resilience you have the better as you will need to entertain children and adults alike for days in a row.

Puppeteer — A puppeteer uses puppets to create an entertainment for an audience. Some will also make their own puppets for their shows. Puppeteers use different types of puppets, including string and hand puppets. Shadow puppets are also popular in many parts of the world. As well as being skilled in animating puppets, you will need to be good at voicing the puppet. Work is available for children's shows, on TV, in amusement parks, in the theatre and for private events.

Circus Performer — Are you born to star under the big top? Make your way across a tightrope? Fly on the trapeze? Juggle, eat fire, clown, train lions or elephants? Then run away and join the circus. People-based circuses are more popular than animal ones in modern Britain and there are plenty of acts for circus people to perform in. Not only in a circus either, but in events or adverts, the entertainment industry needs you. You could even end up using your skills teaching circus workshops – they are popular for corporate team events.

Magician — Maybe you'll end up on the party circuit or you could be a David Copperfield on TV and the international celebrity circuit with a superstar girl/boyfriend. Or if you are not quite as talkative, how about becoming a magician's assistant? You can be right in front of a big audience as you get sawn in half. Try finding out more from The Magic Circle.

Performance Poet — Performance poetry takes place in venues like clubs and pubs across the country. A performance poet will recite poetry (often known as spoken word) out loud to an audience. Poetry may be about politics, human rights or feminism. It may be comic or straight.

VERY COOL

Equestrian — An equestrian is a professional rider who turns riding into an entertainment. They work at circuses but also other horse shows. They are highly skilled and may ride bareback or perform acrobatics on the horses. The Spanish Riding School is world famous for its dancing horses.

Professional Speaker — If you are highly extrovert and have ideas to share, you might want to consider the world of professional speaking. There is a role for speakers who are able to inform and entertain corporate and international audiences. You will need to develop your own niche, work with speakers' bureaus, brand and market your programmes, and learn to tell a good joke!

UBER-COOL

What if you want to be admired by millions? Where, in the past, there were only a handful of stars, now there are A to Z lists of celebrities. Being a celebrity gives you the chance to be seen by millions in magazines, newspapers and on television. It doesn't appear on the surface as if every celebrity has talent, but at the very least it takes a talent for self-publicity and self-branding to get you from the jobs many celebrities started out doing to the doors of Chinawhite or the pages of *Heat* magazine. What jobs should you do if you want to become one?

TV Presenter — With the rise of multi-channel TV, why not try your hand at TV presenting? OK, it's a tough game to get into but, if your personality, energy, enthusiasm and ambition are there, you could be in with a chance. The chemistry is more important than the qualifications. Get yourself noticed through local or hospital radio or acting, volunteer as a runner at a TV production company, or do your research on websites such as PACT.

Model — Modelling is not only a visible career in itself but, with any luck, can lead you on to other professions, such as TV presenting or acting. There are niche jobs for older models, child models and supersize models. Your first port of call should be a model agency. Remember, you'll need a portfolio of photos and you do need to be photogenic.

Stand-up Comedian — Comedians need to be able to keep an audience on their side often late at night, in a club, on a cruise ship or at a private party. It's best to hone your joke-writing skills and develop your comedy routine and persona on the club circuit. Some clubs have an 'open mike' session where you can stand up and see how the audience takes to you. If you start to develop a following then think about approaching a talent agent.

Voice Artist — Professional voice-over and voice artists have developed their vocal qualities – often through dramatic or journalistic training – and use their voices to narrate documentaries, radio, on TV, and in the film industry and for cartoons. They work from a script, which they may sometimes write. They may be employed by a production company or be freelance.

Dancer — What kind of dancer do you want to be? There are opportunities from ballet to ballroom to belly dancing. You can dance full- or part-time, be an instructor, or do ad-hoc TV work. Or how about dancing at a fashion show? It's tough to make a career or money, but think about combining dance with other areas, such as acting. Contact dance associations for details. How about morris dancing, jazz, flamenco, hula, line dancing, jive or hip hop?

* *UNUSUALLY COOL*

Burlesque Performer –

Burlesque derives from the vaudeville tradition and has experienced a big revival in the UK and USA over the last few years. Stars like Dita Von Teese are now headline, big money acts all over the world. Often mistaken for striptease, burlesque is more modest and often comic. As a burlesque performer, you will learn to tease and titillate but never reveal all. Although most performers are women, there are some men on the growing burlesque club circuit. To find out more, dress up in your finest feathers and furs and go and sip champagne with the most glamorous audiences in town.

MOVIE COOL

What could be cooler than the TV and film industry? The media is always popular, and the coolest careers in the industry are the ones where you have the potential to win one of the world's most prestigious awards.

Special Effects — The big budget movies use more and more special effects. Special effects technicians use computer-generated effects and models to create those amazing moments that make the film stand out from the competition.

Screenwriter — The film's director often receives the most accolades for a film, but there wouldn't be a film without a screenwriter. Some famous directors are writer/directors. Other screenwriters have honed their skills on TV or short films. Some screenwriters adapt their own novels.

Director — Many film directors have become household names, but very few make it to the top. Other wannabes stick in TV, the corporate video world, or do a second job while making shorts. If you want to make it to the top, make sure you have both the talent and the self-confidence to sell yourself.

Documentary Maker — TV documentaries are always in demand. Recently, film documentary makers have been all the rage and audiences have flocked to see documentaries in cinemas.

Costume Design — A great costume designer combines imagination with design and research talent. It's not only historical films that need designers; even modern films need a clever wardrobe to set the tone of the movie. They may work closely with the **Hair and Make-up artist.**

Short Film Director/Producer — Short films are a great place to start a film career. They don't take a lot of financing, but expect to do another job for your main salary while you are making yourself a name.

Camera Crew — The camera crews are some of the most highly skilled people in the industry. Cinematography is used to create a unique visual signature for a film. Great cinematography can change our perceptions of a character or location.

Composer — Every film needs someone to write the music and score the picture. There may also be a **Songwriter** involved or even a **Choreographer.**

OSCAR-WINNING COOL

Actor — Clearly every film must have characters. Do you see yourself as the next Judi Dench or Jude Law? Do you have a talent for impersonation? Perhaps you want to be a comic actor or enjoy improvisation or musical theatre. You don't have to go to drama school or train formally, but it may help. Contact agents, network and look at approved drama schools. Get noticed by honing your skills through amateur acting at local theatre groups. Remember to keep your reviews and prepare an audition piece or two.

It is a long hard slog to the top. If you want to know how some of the world's top actors got there, some of their paths are outlined in the celebrity sections.

Six types of actor

1. **The Film/TV/Theatre Star.** You need a big ego, hunger for fame and publicity, and lots of attention from the public as well as talent. Bad news, though – there are less than a hundred who have global recognition. If you want a growth sector in terms of global recognition, head out to Bollywood or check out the Chinese film industry.

2. **Run-of-the-mill Actor.** Acting is more important to you than your salary and ego or you have just never made the big time. You will earn your living through skill but you may never get the fame you deserve.

3. **Character Actor.** From David Jason to Catherine Tate, you can be young or old, and talk in several different accents. You're a real multi-talented artist, always in demand.

4. **Pantomime Horse.** Sometimes it helps to specialise. Be a dame, a horse or a cow. But, beware, your place can be taken by an extra (see below).

5. **Celebrity Actor.** Reality TV can be a route to stardom on the stage, especially in the Christmas season. You could also rake in big cash through commercials and guest appearances.

6. **Extras.** Look at agencies for work as an extra. Surprisingly, being ugly can help. Or having a talent, such as dance. But the pay is poor. You'll have to be motivated by those fleeting few seconds of telly exposure now and again.

12. Different from the rest

I want to have a very unusual career

There are some careers that are so cool that they will make people remember you wherever you go.

Three tips for finding an unusually cool career

1. **Keep your eyes open.** Look in the newspapers, on the internet, on television and in films for interesting careers that other people are doing. There are many new careers out there that didn't even exist a few years ago.

2. **Don't limit yourself.** If you spot a career that someone is doing overseas, don't give up if you can't find the equivalent in this country: you can always set up your own business. Wouldn't it be cool if you were the *only* person in the country doing this cool career?

3. **Get creative.** Think about the type of work you want to do. Don't get hung up on existing job titles. After all, many careers didn't exist a few years ago. Why? Because somebody made up a new job, and the title to go with it. After all, had you ever heard of a house doctor ten years ago? Or would you have thought it possible to make money as a professional lifestyle coach?

You may not want to do any of these, but why not see what ideas they spark off for your own unusual career.

THE UNCONVENTIONAL COOL 100

Here are 100 unusual careers to spark your imagination. Some of the careers speak for themselves and require no explanation, others may be a bit more obscure.

1. **Scrapband maker**
   Why not become a professional instrument maker, making music using scrap metal and used waste materials for music, social and environmental education.
2. **Obsessive Compulsive Disorder expert**
   Obsessive Compulsive Disorder (OCD) is now recognised as a real problem for sufferers. About ten to fifteen per cent of the population apparently have this issue.
3. **Willow worker**
4. **Copper bowl beater**

5. **Wheelwright and wagon builder**
6. **Miniature maker**
    Miniatures have been collectors' items for years. You
    can make a miniature version of anything.
7. **Rice carvers**
    Rice carvers are some of the most skilled of
    professional artists, carving works so small that they
    can only be seen under a microscope.
8. **Truffle Hunter**
9. **Film censor**
    Censors decide what certification should be given to a
    film.
10. **Trainer of 'five rhythms' dance**
11. **Colonic irrigation specialist**
    Colonic irrigation is an alternative practice used to
    support the health of the gut.
12. **Golf ball diver**
    Best make sure the golf club doesn't mind you doing
    this – or even get them to pay you for it.
13. **Doll's house/furniture maker**
14. **Rocking horse maker**
15. **Underwater welder**
16. **Puppet maker**
17. **Alaskan crab fisherman**
    Alaskan crab fishermen work in some of the most
    perilous conditions on earth – in the middle of the
    Bering Sea. The industry is worth big money, though.
18. **Stiltwalker**
19. **Ethnomusicologist**
    A specialist in the music of different cultures.
20. **Fire walk leader**
    Firewalking is a growth industry, teaching motivation in
    the corporate field and for personal development.

21. **Cancan dancer**
22. **Cycling trainer**
    A cycling trainer provides cycle training, sometimes advising on special needs and disabled cycling as well as bike maintenance classes, or bicycle recycling.
23. **Sex toy tester**
    A serious job testing products for durability and other qualities, and, contrary to expectations, not for nymphomaniacs.
24. **Bingo caller**
    With an ageing population, bingo callers are much in demand.
25. **Fingerprint analyser**
26. **Ice sculpture maker**
27. **Forest ranger**
28. **Karate instructor**
29. **Bottom reader**
    It is apparently possible to tell your fortune and character from your bottom.
30. **Lifeguard at a nudist beach**
31. **Ocean scuba guide**
32. **Competition quiz writer**
33. **Sudoku compiler**
34. **Cigar Buyer**
35. **Jewellery designer**
36. **Casting director**
37. **Hotel owner**
38. **Guitar maker**
39. **Personal trainer**
40. **Public policy reseacher**
41. **Nature hike leader**

42. **Animator**
43. **Antiquarian book collector**
   There is a growing market in Chinese books for would-be specialists.
44. **Bookbinder**
45. **Rock climbing guide**
46. **Stenographer**
   A stenographer often works in a court taking notes. Sometimes they provide services for the deaf.
47. **Conflict management counsellor**
48. **Face reader**
   An ancient fortune-telling tradition.
49. **Antiques retailer**
50. **Children's book illustrator**
51. **Architectural photographer**
52. **Park ranger**
53. **Wedding planner**
54. **Music therapist**
55. **TV gameshow host**
56. **Hang-gliding instructor**
57. **Hot rod builder**
58. **Translator of ancient manuscripts**
59. **Body language expert**
60. **Bangra dancer**
   Bangra is the Indian dance form used in Bollywood movies.
61. **Magician's assistant**
62. **Manga (Japanese cartoon) translator**
63. **Sex surrogate**
64. **Deaf signing instructor**
65. **Graphic novelist/cartoonist**

66. **Cowhand**
67. **Shock jock**
    American DJs who give their opinions perhaps rather too freely.
68. **Juvenile offenders' worker**
69. **Natural food shop owner**
70. **Missionary**
71. **Guide dog trainer**
72. **Map maker**
73. **Cowpuncher**
    Cowpunchers herd, castrate and brand cattle, and do other maintenance work on ranches.
74. **Sommelier**
    Picks the wines that will accompany different foods.
75. **Sex trainer**
    Teaches people how to improve their sex lives.
76. **Kilt maker**
77. **Sumo wrestler**
    Sumo has been popular in Japan for hundreds of years.
78. **Professional dowser**
    Looking for geopathic stress, water, leylines or oil.
79. **Lighthouse keeper**
    It is too late to become a lighthouse keeper in the UK – the last one went in the 1990s – but, if you really want to do this job, contact lighthouse associations in other countries.
80. **Wigmaker**
81. **Drystone waller**
82. **Bagpiper**
83. **Acrobat**
84. **Brocade weaver**
85. **Quilt maker**

86. **Candle maker**
87. **Gem polisher**
88. **Bridge designer**
89. **Lavender grower**
90. **Miller**
91. **Orchid hunter**
92. **Club picker**
   A club picker is the person who chooses the lucky people who get to go into a nightclub.
93. **Infomercial maker**
   Direct response advertising is very 21st century. As the producer of an infomercial, you can help to develop concepts and a marketing strategy and then shoot a film with a director.
94. **Professional knitter**
   With homemade becoming cool again, what better way to help others get the look while making a handsome living yourself.
95. **Cowboy boot maker**
   This is a very skilled profession, in which you learn both to make and decorate leather boots.
96. **Monk**
97. **Museum designer**
   There are a number of very specialist design areas in big buildings and landscape features across the world.
98. **Maker of unusual human-powered machines**
   These could include recumbents, pedal boats and work bikes.
99. **Fish farm owner**
100. **Sail maker**
   A highly traditional career now being revolutionised by space age fabrics and the demands of high-tech boat design

Index